the OLD GUIDE REMEMBERS & the YOUNG GUIDE FINDS OUT

the OLD GUIDE REMEMBERS &
the YOUNG GUIDE FINDS OUT

Joe Back and Vic Lemmon

Johnson Books • Boulder

Cover design by Joyce Rossi
Cover Art: "Horses, Hitches & Joe," sculpture by
    R.M. Glomb
Illustrations by Joe Back and Gary Shoop

ISBN 0-933472-99-4

LCCCN 86-81364

Printed in the United States of America by
Johnson Publishing Company
1880 South 57th Court
Boulder, Colorado 80301

To our sweet wives, Mary and Pauline, and our beloved Wyoming mountains. Without them, we couldn't have done it.

CONTENTS

Introduction

My friends, the title of this book has encouraged you to open the pages to see what's in here. If you think this means a lot of blood and thunder you may be sorry—there may be some thunder but not much blood. I'm writing my share of this book years after age made me quit being a big game guide, hunter, and packer. I've already written three books which have been well-received in my estimation, but don't you think I'm James Joyce or Ernest Hemingway. I'm just another creature with a lot of cheap paper and a borrowed pencil. The person at the desk is watching you to see if you are serious about buying this. Are you? Let's both take a chance on that.

Quite a few years ago I made friends with an artist named Thomas Hart Benton, a much greater artist than I could ever be. I knew he'd painted many big murals and was known as one of America's foremost regional painters. I found he'd traveled around to a lot of places I'd only read about. We found that a mutual interest besides art was playing the mouth harp. He was much better than me, had played in bands, but we had a lot of fun together. He found out I was an omnivorous reader. I couldn't spell that big word but I knew what it meant.

Now for years I had harbored a hidden desire to write down some of my adventures guiding hunters and riding horses up and down these rough and rocky mountains, and I hoped some souls would be willing to read the stuff and even pay for what they read. My wife, Mary, and I lived for years near Dubois in this mountain country near Yellowstone Park. We owned some small ranches and quite a few horses off and on. Tom spent some time in one of our cabins, painting and drawing while he visited with us, so he knew all this and quite a lot about my adventures. One day (this was before I'd tried any kind of writing) I confessed to Tom this wish to write, and we fell to talking about art and writing. I felt that Tom, who had been in lots of strange places and among all kinds of people, had plenty of information I could use if I could worm it out of him. He had a great vocabulary. Tom was a very modest man, not a blowhard or bragger, just loved to talk about the things he'd seen and find out about the things I'd seen. He was about fifteen years older than me. I'd been in the first world war and so had he. He was Army and I was Navy.

One day we fell to talking about how to express yourself, and he came up with ideas I never thought of or heard of. Tom was a great smoker (so was I then), but he laid his cigar down and said, "Look, Joe, here is a great big pile of just words, if you want to write. That's all Herman Melville, Victor Hugo, and the rest of them had to work with. And here's several piles of different colors, that's all that Leonardo da Vinci and Michelangelo had, and you can even buy better colors now. If you want to sculpture, all you need is a bunch of clay or wax. That's all that Charlie Russell and Frederic Remington had to work with. It's not the tools or equipment, but what you do with your mind that counts."

I knew Tom was proficient in all these mediums. He even spoke several languages I only had an inkling of. He says, "Now, Joe, you may think I'm stringing you along, but I'm not. The caveman had only rocks to draw on and rocks to draw with, and when he communicated with his tribesmen he could only make noises of different kinds—that we call words now. These men were not too different from us now. They had hopes and fears and joys and sorrows just as we have. You have just as much chance as the caveman or any of the great ones. You have a lot to say, Joe, and I'd like to read it. It's in your mind, but it's not out yet.

"About using those words: before you even start writing, in order to put some of those words in order, you should get a book called Roget's Thesaurus. It may help you a lot."

I love jokes, and I knew Tom did, and I thought he was kidding. I thought some Frenchman named his boy Roget, and Roget had a pet fossil animal. But anyway I wrote the name down and told Mary about it, and one day in a bookstore she found a book by that name and gave it to me. I wouldn't be without it. It straightens out your use of words.

It was several years later that I got up my nerve to try my hand at writing, and once I got started I couldn't stop. This was about twenty-seven years ago. My first book, *Horses, Hitches & Rocky Trails*, came out in 1959 and was a kind of manual to help a human pack all his stuff on an animal so he wouldn't have to carry it. This book was well-received and sold well clear up to now. After it I wrote two other books, *Mooching Moose & Mumbling Men* and *The Sucker's Teeth*. These came out in hardback and paperback and sold for about ten years. In the last few years many friends have urged me to write about my experiences, and here, at the age of eighty-six, I'm going to give it a whirl.

But not alone, this time. I've got a great friend, Vic Lemmon, who is twenty-eight years younger than me. We share a whole lot of the same viewpoints. Like me, he's a sculptor, also a packer, guide, and outfitter, and crazy about these mountains. When I first got to thinking about this book, I told Vic about it, and he got to yarning about some of his guiding experiences. He says, "Maybe you could use some of this in your book." Darned if he isn't one great teller of stories, and, besides, things have changed some in the guiding business. The horses are still the same, but hunting is some different, and Vic is right up on top as an interpreter. I said, "I don't want to use *your* stuff—I want *you* to use your stuff. Let's write this book together." As it turns out, we're each writing half.

Other friends who are helping us include Gary Shoop who is providing the illustrations. He's also a fine sculptor and painter. Then there is Skip Glomb, whose sculpture, "Horses, Hitches and Joe," is on the cover. Skip, besides being known for his sculpture, is also a well-known Wyoming painter. And most of all there's my sweet wife, Mary, transcriber and editor.

So now, here goes:

PART I

THE OLD GUIDE REMEMBERS

By Joe Back

"Horse and Hunter," bronze sculpture by Joe Back.

Coyote

I spent one whole winter on my homestead. I only had to live there a little more than that, because when I filed on it I was just out of the Navy, after World War I, and the government counted Navy time as residence time. This was forty miles north of Douglas, Wyoming, on the Dry Fork of the Cheyenne River. I spent most of my time with a team and wagon, hauling firewood from the cottonwood bottoms of the river, and trapping coyotes. That winter coyote skins sold to the fur-buyer for seven to fifteen dollars.

In April I would have liked to have got a job with my nearest neighbor, Rhea Tillard, so I could have lived on my place, but he said he couldn't use me till later. So I found work as a ranch hand for the Slaughter & Patzoldt Co., fifteen miles up the river. Their brand was Fifty-five Ƨ5. That spring there was word around that some homestead cabins, unoccupied, had been looted. No one guessed who had done it. The homesteaders near me were all good people, mostly ex-soldiers or sailors like me. I figured I'd better store the stuff I had with one of my friends. Jim McLaughlin, older than me, said he had an extra cabin I could use, and he would be living on the place all year.

By this time I'd acquired two horses. My deal with the Ƨ5 included keeping my horses free in one of their big pastures. One morning I put one saddle-horse in my own twenty-acre fenced pasture, saddled up the other, and rode the two miles south to Jim McLaughlin's place. I helped him hitch up his team to his wagon, tied my saddle horse on behind, and rode back with him to gather up my stuff—stove, extra bed, shovel, crowbars, hammer, saws, and other things useful to me, and handy for some robber to pick up.

I got over to Jim's place plenty early, but he already had his team up and fed and watered. Jim's whole working life was spent as a conductor for the Northwestern Railroad. He saved all he could, got a small inheritance, and decided to live the life of Riley on his own land. He filed on his homestead in 1916, just after the 640-acre Stock Raising Homestead Act was passed. He had a big flowing spring on his place and built his cabins close to the spring. From it he watered about twenty acres, to raise hay to feed his team. He never married, saying he wanted to stay a free man. He had two cats, whose job it was to keep mice, packrats and chipmunks away from the house, and he had a big brown dog that, he said with a grin, could whip any grizzly that wanted to come around and kept the coyotes away from his chickens. They were in a tight pen anyhow. Jim called him Pancake, said he was hell on sourdough flapjacks, and it took a lot of flour and jackrabbits to feed them both. Pancake thought his place was right behind the wagon, but my saddle horse was tied there. Pancake did some growling but finally moved for the trip into last place, behind my horse. It took about an hour to get to my place. There wasn't a road, only a two-track trail that led down a deep draw, across a sagebrush flat, and then into my homestead.

Jim told some more yarns about Pancake as I was sitting beside him on the wagon seat. I didn't have to believe them all, because Jim loved a joke. I didn't quite buy the one about Pancake running down an antelope.

We stopped close by my cabin door, and we went to work loading up my gear. We had it pretty well finished when we heard some excited barks. Pancake was fifty yards or so from us, making the dirt fly from his dig. Must have been a badger-hole—there were a lot of them around. The horses were OK and Jim's team was tied to a post, so we walked over to see what Pancake was in to. Jim says, "Hell's Bells! There's another dog helping Pancake!" Jim didn't cuss much, and Hell's Bells! was his favorite swear word. Sure enough, close to Pancake, was another dog with his head out of sight in another badger hole, raising just as much dust and rocks. We wondered out loud, laughing, where the other dog come from. Pancake heard us and backed out and found himself looking right into the grinning face of a coyote, who'd backed out at the same time. With an agonized yelp, Pancake leaped for his helper who danced out across the sagebrush just ahead of a frantic Pancake, who was barking and yelping and telling that coyote what he would do to him if he ever caught him. Pancake, full of fried jackrabbit and flapjacks, fell down three or four times, while his helper danced around him like a tumbleweed, encouraging him to come get him, with little yelps. The chase lasted fifty yards or so, before Pancake had to give up and come limping back to Jim and me, his feet full of cactus.

The coyote followed Pancake back, daring him to come get him, and the dog made several other runs at him. He finally dragged himself panting back and lay down at Jim's feet. We were laughing so hard we had to collapse on the bench by the cabin door. Jim got himself together to pull out some cactus from the dog's feet. The coyote was mostly behind a sagebrush, but we could see his ears and his mouth, and he was laughing, too, with little yips and yelps. Pancake was insulted. He dragged himself over to where he could lie in the shade of the wagon and get his breath.

My plan was to go back with Jim and unload my stuff, and he asked me to have dinner with him. Then I was going to ride my saddle horse back, pack the other horse with the gear I left in my cabin that I'd need for the summer, and take off for the ᴣ5. So I tied my saddle horse back on to Jim's wagon, opened the gate for him and shut it behind him, and got up on the seat by him. Pancake went back to last place. No, not last place, because here came the coyote lightly up behind. Pancake bolted for him, and coyote danced away. Pancake came stubbornly back, and here behind him came coyote. Pancake was getting tired and finally gave up and quit chasing. We must have been at the edge of coyote's territory by then. He quit, too, and we saw him sitting on a little hill watching us.

You know, I never could trap coyotes after that one.

Hunting Elk at Midnight

I'd spent the whole fall guiding hunters for an outfit and came out of the deal with a nice, fat cow elk, the best meat I'd ever tasted. I owned a homestead, 640 acres forty miles north of Douglas, where I intended to winter five or six horses that I'd traded for during my hunting trips. This was about a month before Christmas. Before I could take my horses down, I had to check them over and re-shoe some of them. This was going to be a long, hard trip, about 300 miles.

I needed a place to stay, and Jack Gabart invited me to stay with him. He was an old friend of mine, about thirty years older than me. He had about an acre of land right in the middle of Dubois, a good cabin, and a barn and big corral where he kept a couple horses of his own. His place bordered on Horse Creek, so he had access to water, which remained open most of the winter. Jack used to be a teamster for the Tie Camp, the Wyoming Tie and Timber Company, along with Grizzly Bill Murray. If my memory serves me right, this is what happened during the month and a half I stayed with him, in the winter of 1924-25.

He had spent most of his life in the mountains. Jack and I were heavy meat eaters. I had given away a quarter of my elk to a friend before I moved in with Jack, and by now most of the rest of that fat cow was eaten up. We were beginning to get a little bit meat-hungry. We had plenty of hay and grain for our horses, but for ourselves we were shy on meat, and we'd talked about it several times.

At night, after we'd eaten and cleaned up the supper dishes, we usually played checkers or read until maybe 9 or 9:30, when we hit the hay. Jack had a comfortable warm cabin, wood stove, and plenty of firewood. One night he said "We're going to stay up till about midnight tonight, then we're going elk hunting."

I thought Jack had suddenly lost most of his marbles, so I got me a

10

chunk of stove wood for protection, and got behind the stove before I said, "What do you mean, Jack, hunting elk at midnight?" Jack set down his coffee cup, gave me a long laugh and said, "You won't need that chunk of stove wood. You won't even need that '95 Winchester you've been toting around ever since I've known you."

This was one of the coldest nights I'd ever seen in December. It was very cloudy but hadn't snowed yet. He got out his checkerboard, and as usual beat me three or four games, and by then it was close to midnight. I was still doubting whether Jack had all the equipment he was born with; but he was much older than me, had been around a long time, and had already shown me he knew stuff I hadn't even heard of. Now he said, "You got some warm wool pants on. Put on your warmest coat and that wool Scotch cap you're always braggin' how warm it is." Jack put on his fur cap and his heavy sheepskin coat and his mittens and pulled his flashlight out from under his pillow. He put a couple fresh sticks in the stove, closed down the dampers, and turned down the coal-oil lamp a little bit, but we still had some light. He said to me, "Ask me no questions and I'll tell you no lies. Keep that flashlight in your pocket unless I ask for it. Don't you say a word and keep right behind me." He opened the door, and I followed him out and closed it behind me.

I wondered if Jack had some tricks I didn't know up his sleeve. He was my host. I was no lawbreaker, I thought, and neither was Jack.

This was a mud road in those days. It was about 100 yards to the highway, which had recently been graveled. Jack wore heavy rubber packs and wool socks, and so did I, so we didn't make much noise. We turned and walked up the street, past Walt Millard's pool hall. There were buildings on both sides, not a light in any of them, and of course in those days there were no street lights. No owl hooted and no dog barked, but I tell you fellows I could have bitten off the tip of my heart every step I took, I was that scared. I stayed far enough behind Jack not to step on his heels, but I was plenty close. I thought, "Jack don't have a gun, and neither do I. This is the most peculiar elk hunt I've ever been on."

We passed the old Ramshorn, a two-story wooden hotel, where the Standard Station in Dubois is now. (It burned down in 1935.) We turned right just beyond it and Jack stopped. He said, in a low mumble so I could barely hear him, "Well, here we are. We'll see what we got, right here and now." Right by us were several piles of corrugated iron roofing. Jack murmured, "Let's have that flashlight." He picked up a piece of roofing by a corner, lifted it up high so I could see when he turned the flashlight on it. There was a fine, fat quarter of bull elk. "Hell, that ain't fat enough!" he said, and dropped it with a clatter. I'll swear, fellers, that I jumped six and a half feet off the ground, and while I was coming down, Jack picked up a corner of another piece of roofing, under which was another fat hind quarter of elk. Still no dog howled, no owl hooted, no light came on. But my heart was still in my mouth. Jack picked up the corner of a third piece of roofing and looked under it quite a spell. "Hell, that's the finest hind quarter of elk I ever see. Joe, you pull that out from under and put it on your shoulder, and we'll go back to camp. Our elk hunt's over."

Jack must have known I was about to have heart failure, because he let that piece of roofing down real careful. We went back the way we'd come, me with that frozen quarter of elk on my shoulder. It must have weighed about 150 pounds or more. But I was young and husky, and the weight didn't bother me as much as the fright did. We got back to the cabin and opened the door before my heart settled back into its usual rhythm. Jack said to me as he shut the door behind me, "Just put it down on the floor. It's froze hard as hell and it'll be all right." We were plenty tired. We shucked off our outside clothes, got into our bedrolls, and Jack blew out the light. He locked the door first. I didn't sleep very well. I had bad dreams about our midnight elk hunt.

I didn't know whether we were poachers or thieves. Those elk quarters were sure outdoors in the open—we didn't do any breaking and entering. Nobody in Dubois had electricity in those days. There were no refrigerators, and you had to keep your meat where it would stay coldest. Poachers sounded better than thieves to me. I was hungry, and we had our meat, so that's the way I put it in my own mind.

In the morning, Jack got out his meat saw and sawed off a couple of steaks, while I got out his sourdough pot and stirred up some flapjacks. We already had some raisins cooked up, so we had a feast. Jack had me take out the quarter and hang it up in an old shed by his barn that he used for a meathouse. Before I did that, he sawed off a few three- or four-pound chunks to thaw for roasts.

We had a very fine breakfast, fed the horses, and Jack said, "Let's go over to Walt Millard's pool hall and see if maybe we can beat old Judge Green at a game of pool."

Judge Green had lost quite a lot of his eyesight. He had a lot of white whiskers. He and his son Ollie had come from the Hamilton, Montana, country and built up a fine cow ranch about where the Parker Ranch is now located. The judge must have been born with a pool cue in his hand, because, small as he was and poor as his sight was, I'd never seen him beaten in a game of pool. After he'd beat Jack Gabart a couple of games, Jack turned over his pool cue to me, and said, "Let's see you beat the judge. I'll bet you an elk steak you can't do it." After the judge had beat me three games, he slapped me on the back, wiggled his whiskers, and asked, "Are there any other suckers around ready for a whirl?" There were only two or three other guys there, and the judge had already beaten them, so while I paid for my games they only grinned and went on visiting. I was getting braver by then. I bought a couple of cigars, gave one to the judge, and lit up my own. Jack packed up his pipe and said, "Joe, I'm gettin' kinda hungry, let's go back to the cabin."

An old timer came in the door just then, a friend of mine that I'd guided with and packed with that fall. He came over to me and whispered, "Joe, have you seen anybody packin' any elk around, last night or the night before?"

By nature I'm not a thief or a liar, but he had me this time. I had to lie a little. "No, Erl," I said, "I haven't seen anything like that." Of course, I really hadn't. That quarter was on my shoulder, and I couldn't see it.

So, I knew I was a poacher, all right, but a second-hand poacher. The Ramshorn Hotel must have been buying poached elk, and calling it "beef" when they served it. I got my horses put in pasture down country and got me a job shovelling hay. That was the last time I hunted elk at midnight.

Snipe Hunting

One winter I was offered a good job shovelling hay at the Morton Ranch out of Douglas, Wyoming. Cannon was their brand. Good pay—$55 a month, they furnished everything, and the food was great, so I took it. All you needed were good warm clothes, a good bedroll, and a willingness to work hard. Looked like it was going to be a hard winter. Jack ran a good spread and wouldn't ask any of the hands to do anything he wouldn't do. There were two men to each hayrack, and the haystacks were in different pastures. One man would drive the team, the other spread the hay, and we'd take turns. This was irrigated land, so we had to drive across a good many laterals. The bunkhouse was big, bunks built two- or three-high, one above the other. It could hold fifteen men, and it was filled in haying time. As I remember, this was a pretty tough winter, and a lot of hay and cottoncake fed to the cows. All the work was done by horses as there were very few pickups or trucks.

There were three or four Mexicans working on the ranch, and in two or three months I learned enough Spanish so I could get along with them pretty good. Most of them could speak some English. One of the Mexicans was a good-looking young fellow with a pleasant personality who seemed to know very little English. We young fellows were mostly in our early twenties and felt sure we knew it all. After work, if we weren't too tired, we'd play some games. The ranch didn't allow poker so we played checkers a lot, and the young fellow I mentioned (his name was Johnny) beat me at checkers every time.

One fine moonlight night, a bunch of us young fellows decided we should show Johnny what life was all about; we should take him snipe-hunting. He said, "Don't know snipe, amigos. Sure like to learn." A couple of us went out to the storehouse and got a big wool sack and a couple of kerosene lanterns. We made sure the lanterns were full of kerosene and the wicks were well-trimmed. We also carried out some stakes with a couple of big ones being about four feet long. We divided up the load, Johnny carrying his share. There were several barb-wire fences to cross, kind of a job with the load, especially because it was cold and we were wearing heavy wool pants and big coats and fur or wool caps. But we finally made it without too many snags to a sagebrush hill beyond the fields. We found a little square spot, about twenty-five feet on a side, with not too much sagebrush, to set up the snipe trap. A wool sack is gunnysacking about eight feet long and with a wide opening, used to stack wool in at sheep-shearing time.

Johnny was very cooperative and helped wherever he could. We gave him directions in what we called pidgin-Mexican. We staked the wool sack out, with a couple of the long stakes added to spread it open as a trap to catch the snipe. We crumbled up some left-over flapjacks, made a trail of them up to the wool sack, and left a pile of crumbs inside. We scraped out a little flat place on each side of the wool sack, one for each lantern and lit them. We told Johnny to station himself three or four feet behind the snipe trap and every few minutes to holler "Who-who-who-who-who-who" in a low monotonous voice.

We hadn't had much trouble getting ready. The cook, when we begged the flapjacks, said he'd like to have a bunch of snipe to cook up. Jack Morton, the boss, said that was all OK, provided we brought back the wool sack, stakes and lanterns when the hunt was over. Jack, who spoke fluent Spanish, had a little talk with Johnny before we left the cookhouse. As we understood it, he was helping us out by telling Johnny about the ways of snipes.

We fellows spread out on each side, walking down the hill and hollering kind of low, "Who-who-who-who-who," and we could hear Johnny, up on the hill, hollering back, "Who-who-who-who." It took us an hour or so to get down off the sagebrush hill and across the fields and fences back to the bunkhouse. We lit the two lamps and stoked up the stove and stood around, taking off our clothes and laughing about how we'd taught that Mexican how we do things in the U.S. We hadn't ever played out this joke before, but we were enjoying it.

The other Mexicans were all in bed with the soogans over their faces. I did notice one peeking out with a grin. We closed up the dampers on the stove and were turning down the lamps, when we heard giggles from the top bunk. It was Johnny. He'd beat us down and got his bed all warmed up, while waiting for us snipe hunters. Johnny said, "No snipe come in. Maybe tomorrow morning they be there. You savvy snipe?"

15

We didn't have a word to say right then. We blew out the lamps and climbed into bed. I said, "Goodnight, Johnny, you smart son-of-a-gun." Johnny just giggled a little more.

In the morning we hay-haulers got into our warmest clothes and went out and fed and watered our teams. We heard the cook holler, "Come 'n' git it or I'll throw it out!" So as soon as we could we piled into the cookhouse. The Mexicans were all grinning, especially when the cook remarked, "Where are all those snipe I was counting on for dinner?" We knew then that we were six U.S. boys that had been jobbed. We still had to fit into our hay-hauling day the getting back the wool sack, stakes, and lanterns.

We found out later that Johnny's father was a friend of Jack's down in Arizona and that Jack had given him this job so he could learn the cow business, and that Johnny had more education than any of us, including our boss, Jack. We also found he could laugh in about six languages.

Thereafter, on Saturday nights all winter when we went into Douglas for a little fun (it was prohibition, then, and you couldn't *legally* drink), some clerk or somebody would be sure to say, "How are the snipe at the Cannon Ranch?" I never took anybody else snipe hunting, because I got a good education that night.

Shorty and His Spud-Hole

This story is about a man who was one of the best cooks I ever met in a hunting camp. As every hunter knows, if he hunts in a cold mountainous country, a spud-hole is dug in the back of the cook tent to protect potatoes and other vegetables from freezing. This fine cook was Shorty Bell. At this time of year, chipmunks would sometimes try to make a home in the spud-hole. Shorty would never admit it, but he loved all animals. He'd chase the chipmunks out, but he'd help them on their way with bread crumbs.

This camp was a spike camp that was off five or six miles from the main camp, and the site had been used for several years, on permit from the U.S. Forest Service. Camp had just been set up: the wall tents for the hunters, tipi tents for the guides, and the cook tent. The spud-hole had been dug, and we were all out looking for game when this happened.

We had a good table, made several years before, in the center of the cook tent. Shorty's stove was, as usual, to your right as you came in. Shorty usually rolled his bed out over the loose boards that covered the spud-hole—extra insulation to keep stuff from freezing. Shorty was a pretty fussy housekeeper, so if you didn't put things where they belonged you got hell from Shorty. I guess this time he forgot he hadn't yet boarded up the spud-hole when he needed some water. He grabbed the pail from the pile of groceries that weren't put away yet, made a misstep, fell into his own spud-hole, and sprained his left ankle.

About eight or ten inches of snow had fallen in the last few days, but now it was warm and sunny, and the snow was starting to go off. These tents were set up about 150 feet from the creek that drained Terrace Mountain, sometimes called Terrace Creek and sometimes Fremont County Line Creek. This was in a small, beautiful grassy park. Shorty got

17

his water supply from a fine big spring that came out from under the roots of a spruce tree, a big one, about 100 feet from the cook tent. Over the years a path had been worn to it through the sagebrush, grass, and rocks.

When we came back in the afternoon, we found Shorty with his left ankle bound up, sitting by the stove getting supper for the crew. When we saw this we kidded Shorty and asked him if a big bull elk had run through camp and run over him. Shorty gave us a long story about how he'd sprained his ankle in the spud-hole, defending himself at every step against possible charges that he'd been careless in his housekeeping. As a cook is the most valuable man in a hunting camp, we believed every word he said, until he got going about himself and a moose. According to Shorty, after he got his ankle tied up, he hobbled down to the spring. As he was stooping down to fill the water pail, he heard some odd snuffling and found himself looking right into the eyes of the biggest bull moose he ever saw, with his head lowered to get some water, too.

Shorty was afraid to make a move. He let go the bail of the water pail, and slowly edged over behind the big spruce, putting it between himself and the moose. Shorty said he peered around the trunk, and the moose was still there, staring at Shorty. Shorty said that just for the hell of it he reached out his hand and arm, and petted the moose on the end of his huge bulbous nose. The moose didn't make a single move until he got the whiff of Shorty's hand stroking his nose. He gave a couple of rolling snorts, whirled around, crossed the creek, and disappeared into the timber on the other side. Shorty said his hands were clean, but the moose couldn't stand the smell anyway.

Shorty said, "By the grins you damn fools got on your mugs, I know you don't believe this, but I got so weak I had to sit down behind the tree and just wait for ten or fifteen minutes to make sure he wasn't coming back. When I finally got my nerve back, I got the pail of water and hobbled back to the tent, just about an hour before you fellows showed up." He took us out, hobbling, and showed us the very fresh tracks of man and moose in mud and snow, so of course we told him we believed every word he said.

That night, after we had grained and taken care of our horses, belled them all, and the horse wrangler had taken them out on good grass on the hill across the creek, we put a couple of horses on picket for the morning's wrangle. Shorty called us in to supper, "Come 'n' git it!" The cook tent was in perfect housekeeping order. The boards were over the spud-hole and Shorty's bed over the boards. Supper conversation carefully avoided spud-holes, for awhile. Some careless soul asked Shorty, "Bet you'll watch your spud-hole after this!" He flared right up. "If I hear any more guff about spud-holes I'll put that guy in the spud-hole, cover him up, and leave him there all winter!"

Bellyachin Lin

I knew Bellyachin Lin a long time ago. This is a story about a man who was a complaining sort. He was a pretty good hand, was well-educated, came from a wealthy cattle-raising family, but had this regular nickname, Bellyachin Lin.

This was no cow outfit we were on. It was a dude spread, taking summer parties on pack trips into the high mountains. The boss of our party was an old-timer named John Hough, who'd been up the creek and over the mountain plenty of times already. Lin's job was horse-wrangler and packer's assistant and general helper around camp. My job was horse-wrangler's helper and cook. I wasn't very much of a cook, but the meals seemed to go down all right, with no complaints except from Bellyachin Lin.

The reason we were all working for this outfit was the pay. Ordinary ranch wages in those days were fifty to sixty dollars a month, but here the pay was princely—$100 a month. Oh, the hours were long—seven days a week, sunup to sundown, and sometimes longer. We were camped on the South Fork of the Buffalo, the weather was wonderful, and you couldn't beat the fishing. That's what the five dudes in our camp were interested in.

Every three or four days we would move camp ten or fifteen miles into a different stretch of country, for different fishing, or for new views for the dudes' cameras. They all seemed to be camera experts and had plenty of the most modern gear. John Hough and I didn't know the first thing about cameras, but Lin billed himself as an expert and would talk at length about his expertise. One of the dudes told me privately that Lin didn't know any more about cameras than a horse knew about the moon. John Hough and I could see we were heading into trouble.

John was the boss and a fine boss to work for. As long as you did your job, he didn't criticize; he would help with any job; he didn't talk much, but he was always friendly and courteous. He was especially handy with horses, and we had a lot of good horses, pack and saddle horses both. All the equipment was first class—nobody with any savvy could criticize any of it. But Lin criticized anything and everything.

Lin was raised in the Powder River country near KC. He was well-acquainted with the rattlesnakes, greasewood, sagebrush, and grass of that part of the state; but he contrived to make himself an expert about the high mountains, too, and something about them never suited him. He was always the last to crawl out of his bedroll in the morning, and he always crawled out grumbling. Something was always wrong with the weather—it was raining, or there was snow in the air, or the wind came from the wrong direction.

One of the things that bothered us was that he had the worst case of the "gimmies" that I ever saw. If you were a smoker, and I was, when he'd see you light up he'd ride up with two fingers extended, saying, "Gimme," and the easiest thing to do was put a cigarette between those fingers. If he saw the Bull Durham hanging out of your pocket, he'd stay away as he didn't like to roll his own. And since the hands mainly rolled 'em, it was mostly the dudes he was bothering. Once in a while, back at the ranch, when I was feeling flush, I'd buy me a few packages of tailor-mades, and sure enough, here would be Bellyachin Lin with his fingers extended, saying "Gimme!"

© gary Shoot

21

I was in the corral putting pack saddles on some horses, ready to move camp again, when John Hough came over to me. In an undertone he said, "I'm getting damn tired of this over-educated Bellyachin Lin. Nothin' suits him. The dudes are getting all-fired tired of him. Most of them move away when they see him comin'. I'm pretty near at the point of tellin' him to pack up his stuff and go back to the ranch. But then, it's only a few days till this trip's over. Can we stand it that long? What do you think, Joe?"

I said, "We've stuck it out this long, maybe we can take it six or seven days longer. Maybe Lin'll see folks backin' off and get the point. I just don't know. We'll be kind of short-handed if we turn him loose."

John said, "I'll try to stand him as long as I have to. I'll be damn glad to see the last of that jackass. I can hardly stand to say a word to the damn fool."

That's how it came about that I had to be the middleman—the interpreter between those two. It was about the toughest job I ever had.

We got the packsaddles on the horses, got the camp torn down, the rubbish buried deep, the panniers weighed and loaded on the saddles, the tents and beds loaded on top, the saddle horses ready, and we took off for Crater Lake, all the while pretending to pay no attention to Lin who was grumbling all the time.

That day we took off from the camp near Bridger Lake and climbed Woodward Canyon to the Buffalo Plateau, past Ferry Lake on top, and then down the steep trail to Crater Lake, where we thought the fishing ought to be mighty good. Crater Lake is a big lake and is in a deep bowl from the Buffalo Plateau. It looks as if it must be the source of the Soda Fork of the Buffalo, but no surface stream runs out of it. The rim of the bowl goes all the way around, though it is lower on the Soda Fork side. In those days, which were long ago, we never found any other parties when we came there. We could stay five or six days for some glorious fishing. We got there in late afternoon. The dudes got out their fishing gear and went down to the lake, while we got about setting up the special Crater Lake camp.

Lin had never been here before, but John Hough and I had camped here several times and knew more than he did about what we were getting into. The campground had been used by our parties and others over a long time. It was neat and clean, but what counted was a good-sized pile of poles and even some pretty big short logs, off to one side. We started with the cook tent first—it's always the most important one. We had a very good one, a big 12x16 with four-foot side walls, and a big heavy fly to go over the top. John and I rolled two heavy logs over against the sides and tied extra ropes to the logs and the tent sides and over the ridgepole.

Lin's eyes were getting bigger. "What's all that extra work for?" he asked. John Hough said to me, "Joe, you tell that damn fool about Crater Lake and what he's gettin' into."

So I told him. "This is sure pretty country, Lin, but it's more than pretty. It's windy. There's a reason people lugged in all those poles and logs. This is a real crater—that's how it got its name. The wind that comes in here is williwaws. It comes down most any time of day or night. It's a whirlwind. As it goes round and round inside the crater it seems to go faster and faster and finally it seems to come right up out of the ground. You have to tie everything up as strong as the devil or you'll lose it."

"Doesn't make sense to me," said Lin, "We put camp up good an' stout all the time."

"Well, hell," I said, "you put up your own outfit the way you want it. But don't say I didn't warn you."

Lin had a good stout teepee to himself. I slept in the cook tent, like most camp cooks do. At the start of the trip, John shared Lin's tipi, but now he rolled his bed out in the cook tent with me, and Lin had this eight-foot tipi to himself.

This wasn't an Indian tipi. These roundup tipis are four-sided tents made of four triangles of strong canvas, sewed to a peak in the middle, with a strong loop lashed into the peak, and a canvas floor. You can pitch them with a pole in the middle and stakes driven in the corners; or you can lash two poles together like a fence-buck, lash the peak of the tipi to the pole-crossing, drive in the corner stakes, and push it up into position. These tipis have been used in hunting camps and round-up camps for many years.

While Lin went off to settle his own difficulties, John and I really anchored down the cook tent, adding logs to front and back, lashing ropes with strong half-hitches over the ridge-pole and to the logs and to extra stakes. It would take some cyclone to undo our job. We also extra-wired the chimney to the tent, put rocks under the stove, and wired the stove to the rocks, ready for all hell to break loose, if it should. John grinned at me and said, "If this comes along, maybe that intellectual monstrosity will add another degree to his education."

Then we got after the gear tent and the dudes' tipis, first setting them up as usual, then adding extra logs and ropes to weigh them down. Lin helped, doing what he was told, but grumbling all the while. I had to quit to get supper when the dudes came up with their big mackinaw trout. They were really happy about the place and the fishing, taking pictures of the fish and each other and saying, "This is the best part of our trip."

Before dark we took care of the horses. We put three saddle horses on picket, on good grass near camp. Two we staked out, making real sure the stakes were strong and were driven in deep. The third one we picketed to a good big short log in an open space, so if he got scared and ran, he would have to drag that log. We made that deal a little sure by picketing one foot, with half a hobble, to the log. I knew this particular horse was well picket-broke—I'd done it myself. I was sure he'd not get tangled up, whatever happened. The rest of the horses we ran out on a meadow close to the lake.

We visited awhile in the cook tent after supper. One after another the dudes got sleepy and turned in. Then Lin went off to his tent, and John and I rolled out our beds in the cook tent. It was cold outside, and the fire was about out in the stove. John said, "I don't believe I'll build it up any—let it go out till morning."

We could hear some snores as we settled down. Sometime along in the night I woke up to the sound of the wind. As I listened, I heard John say, "I think it's startin' for a williwaw." Sure enough the wind got stronger and louder, and the trees began to creak and whistle. We could hear people talking in the dudes' tents and the horses snorting. The stovepipe began rattling against the wires holding it down. Along came a bigger and louder gust of wind, and the chimney came apart. Some smoke came into the tent, but the pipe still held tight where it was tied onto the stove and went through the roof-jack. We heard a wild yell outside, from the direction of Lin's tipi, just as the bottom section of stovepipe ripped away from the stove and made screaming noises as the billowing canvas scrunched it over the stove top. Smoke filled the inside of the tent. I sat up. John's voice came quietly: "Lie down, Joe. No smoke next to the ground. We can't do a thing till the wind goes down. I didn't know Lin could make such a loud noise. We know he ain't dead, he's moanin' and groanin' too much, an' we can't do a thing for him now. We gotta wait."

About 12 or 1 o'clock, the wind changed its tune—quit screaming and started sighing. The smoke in the cook tent sort of settled, since the fire had gone out; so John and I got up, pulled on our pants, boots, coats, and hats, dug out our flashlights and went out to see what was up. The moon was out, and the wind had just about gone down.

John said, "I'll fix up the chimney and get a fire started. Joe, you go check on Lin. I think the dudes are OK and back asleep—no sound out of them."

There wasn't any sign of Lin's tipi. But he called to me, and I found him over near the gear tent, scrunched up in a couple of pack covers, trying to keep warm, "Are you hurt, Lin?" I asked him. He unrolled a little and started stretching out arms and legs. He was just in his underwear and showed a lot of bruises and scratches. He pulled the pack covers back over himself again. "Man!" he said, "I sure wish I'd listened to you guys who knew something about this!" That was the first time I ever heard him run himself down and give somebody else credit. I wanted to hear more. "Tell me about it, Lin."

"Well," he said, "the whole tipi came up in the air with me in it, and dumped me and the bedroll right out of the opening. I rolled a ways, and the rolling was getting me out of the bedroll. I tried grabbing the blankets, but the wind pulled them right out of my hands and took them away. I found the wind landed me right up against the front of the gear tent. But the wind was too strong for me to do anything but just lay there. When it went down some I could paw around inside and get these pack covers, but they ain't very warm." He shivered some more.

"Just hang tight a little, Lin," I told him. "John's getting a fire going, and I'm sure we got some clothes we can share with you." I took off my own jacket and wrapped it round him. Hell, it wasn't even freezing, quite, and I had a wool shirt on.

"I gotta go see about the horses," I said, "and if they're OK I'll be back in a little bit."

One of the picket horses was gone. He'd pulled his stake and run off with the lead rope. It was a long stake—I was sure the horse would be tangled up nearby, probably with the main bunch. The other two were snorting and wild-eyed, but they were still picketed OK and hadn't hurt themselves. By moonlight and flashlight I picked my way down to the meadow where the main bunch was supposed to be. It looked to me like they were all there and all right. Even the horse dragging the stake was there, the other horses keeping well away from him, so as not to get tangled in his rope. I just left him there till morning. Nothing more I could do until daylight, so I stopped by the dudes' tents.

Their tents were all right. They said the wind had billowed them plenty, but they were all calmed down now. I tightened up some ropes that had loosened and told them what I knew of the history of these williwaws. Would there be any more tonight? "Just couldn't tell you," I said. "Might as well stay prepared. But if the tents have taken this one this good, I don't think you need to worry."

Lin was at the cook tent. John still wasn't talking to him, and he wasn't saying a word either—just sitting on a hunk of firewood as close to the stove as he could get. He was still dressed in just his long johns and boots and my jacket. He'd washed up some and it looked like he wasn't badly damaged. John had the stove all fixed up, but it took him longer than he expected. You see, we carried five or six lengths of stovepipe that fitted inside the oven when we were traveling. The cook tent had a roof-jack of sheet metal that was laced into it and would shed water. Two lengths of pipe went from the stove into the bottom of the roof-jack, and the rest we jammed on top of each other on the top of the roof-jack when we set up the tent. That was all we had to do if the wind didn't blow; but it generally did, so we tied the chimney to the roof-jack with baling wire every time, and John had done a triple job of tying it all down this time. It came apart anyway, it still wasn't in bad shape, and John just had to straighten out some bent spots and tighten up all the wires.

Now, John had a good fire going and was making coffee. The water pail hadn't tipped over, somehow or other.

We spent some time that day hunting for Lin's tipi. Finally located it high up in a tree, and Lin himself climbed up and brought it down—not in too bad shape, but with a few rips to sew up. Never did find the blankets; they must be in Crater Lake. We used the spare bedroll for Lin, the one we always took along just in case.

Well, from that time on, Lin sure improved. I sure wish I could say he was a changed man, but he wasn't changed all that much. He was always good with horses, and from that day he spent more time with them and talked more to them. He sure didn't complain as much, and his extended fingers and his "Gimmee" changed into "Hey, you got a spare?"

Too Much Beer

This happened in a camp I was working in—I'll never forget it. Sort of a super camp—fine location, tents, cook, guides, grass, horses, hunters—all except for one damn fool who had to drink beer in the middle of the night and ruin all the next day's hunting.

We took turns wrangling horses, and had very little horse trouble. Most of the hunters were after elk with big heads. Not many deer in this area, but one hunter was very happy with a mule deer with a big head. We had a bunch of experienced hunters, good-natured, easy to get along with, all non-residents, mostly from the oil country of Texas and Oklahoma.

The whole camp got up early and started out about daylight, all mounted on strong, fat horses. This was on the South Fork of the Buffalo in the Terrace Mountain country. We had a long day hunting and came back to camp hungry, tired, and looking for a rest. We wrangled horses and put them on rich grassy pasture, having already fed them a bait of oats. We put two horses on picket, got down an ample supper, and hit the bedrolls, ready for a night's sleep.

It snowed two or three inches that night. Two hunters were in each tent, with their bedrolls and a little stove. We were all asleep when the damnedest hullaballo broke out about midnight. Except for it, there were only the peaceful sounds of horse bells up on the slopes, the best sound of all to a horse wrangler, because you know they're all close by and happy. This horrible sound we heard came from one of two good friends using the same tent, and we thought they had been getting along fine.

We found out later that one was an avid beer-drinker who had to have a couple of bottles in the middle of the night to help him go to sleep. His friend was a non-drinker, and he got irritated at the getting up, grunting, moving around, getting the drinks before settling back in his bedroll. This bird was a real wag with a great sense of humor, and he framed his friend.

27

The beer drinker had an empty gallon fruit can under his cot to pee in. The non-drinker knew this, of course, and used a trick we'd never have thought of. He borrowed a nail and a hammer from the cook, and pounded three or four holes close to the bottom rim of the pee-pot. Most of us slept in our underwear and a few had pajamas. This night was very cold— about 9000 feet altitude is no part of the tropics.

What caused all the uproar was that the drinker had got out of his bedroll and drunk a bottle of beer, and had to turn loose his flood into his pee-can. We heard his howl when the holes in his pee-can, turned just right, kind of flooded out his middle. He howled like bloody thunder, "Oh, my God, it's frozen and I broke it off and I'm bleeding to death! Somebody come help me!"

He woke up the whole camp. The cook and some of the guides and hunters, and I was one of them, came running barefooted in the sub-zero cold and snow. It was an hour and a half before the camp got through laughing, got their boots and coats on and fires built in their tent stoves, and got back in their bedrolls. The whole rest of the night you could hear grunts and giggles about the damn fool who had to drink in the middle of the night.

Diamond G Camp on Soda Fork

One time I hired out as horse wrangler for the Diamond G Ranch on Brooks Lake, for their hunting camp on Soda Fork. Turned out they had more hunters than guides, couldn't find another one to hire, and so turned me into a guide, even though I didn't have a guide license. As I remember, a man named Jack was the cook. Jules Farlow and Charlie Replogle from Lander were guides and so was my friend Larry from Dubois, a very good man with horses. We had four hunters, most of them from Michigan, as I remember.

The Soda Springs flowed near our camp into the Soda Fork of the Buffalo and gave that fork its name. On its bank was a big cabin owned by the Forest Service, which we used as cook tent, and the hands slept in it. We had two wall tents for the hunters right back of the cabin. As I remember, we had about thirty horses in our string, and we grazed them on Soda Mountain just above the springs. This was in the middle twenties; Terrace Mountain, south of Soda Fork, was closed to hunting until 1934, so we hunted Soda Fork up to Crater Lake above its head. We also hunted on Joy Peak and the valley of Joy Creek, and even on the North Fork of the Buffalo, clear up to Enos Mountain.

We guides each had one hunter. The one that fell to me was a good guy to get along with, but an absent-minded sort who always rode with a very loose rein, which got him into a lot of trouble. I urged him to stay all the time as close to me as he could, so if I saw any game he could see it, too. But he was forgetting all about elk and just admiring the beautiful snow-capped mountains around, while his horse took advantage and stopped to graze. Sometimes he'd be forty to sixty feet behind me.

One day we were on fresh elk sign and tracks. I turned back to motion him to come up, but he wasn't in sight. Just about then he started hollering. I rode fast to see what was up. His horse had walked between two trees, far enough apart for the horse, but too close together for the rider's knees and his saddle. As usual, the ends of the reins were in his hand, and he hadn't reacted to shorten the reins and pull the horse back. I had to do that for him. The horse backed out OK, but the hunter's knees were so damaged that we had to go back to camp. I tied up both ponies, and Jack, the cook, and I had to help the hunter off the horse and get off his boots, trousers, and underwear. We laid him out on his cot, soaked his knees with hot towels for awhile, put on some Absorbine, Jr., and left him to recuperate. It was a couple of days before he could get on a horse again.

His knees were still sore enough that I had to help him mount, but he seemed comfortable riding. We were hunting over on Joy Creek when we saw this big bull elk, all alone. The hunter had his reins more in mind, this time, and he was with me. We dismounted carefully, and the elk just stayed there. I coached him about his rifle, and he took careful aim and shot. The elk flinched, fell down, then jumped up and ran. We led our horses along his trail. He was bleeding pretty bad, so there was no trouble following. The hunter forgot all about his sore knees, he was that excited. Well, we came on the elk, dead, but stuck in the V-fork of a twin lodgepole pine—one that had two trunks from one root, spreading at an angle. I hadn't come on anything just like this before. I kidded the hunter about the elk trying the same trick that his own horse had, two days before.

I always carried a throw rope on my saddle. I tied it around these fine six-point horns. Then, between the hunter and me fussing around, and a pull or two from the horses, it wasn't long before we had the elk laid out on the ground, where I could dress him out.

This was such a beautiful head that the hunter decided he wanted to have a taxidermist do a shoulder mount, so I had to do a careful caping out. In a case like this you never cut the elk's throat, or make any cuts on the lower side in front of the legs. You cut down the back of the neck, from between the ears to back of the withers, and carefully skin out the whole neck and the head, being especially cautious around the eyes, lips, ears, and nose.

I then cut the meat in quarters, using the handaxe I always carried on my saddle. The hunter helped me lay the meat on dry branches, and we broke off pine branches to cover the meat, the cape, and the horns until I could get back with two pack horses in the afternoon to carry everything in to camp.

After I got it all in and the quarters hung on the meat pole, I did a good job scraping out the inside of the cape and salted it and rolled it up ready to pack in to the ranch. The other hunters and their guides came in and put their horses with ours in the corral, all except Larry and his hunter. It was supper time by now, and we all began to get concerned.

It was getting dark, so we started supper, thinking they might be just a little late, when Larry's hunter rode up and jumped off, letting his reins drop, and told us, all out of breath, "Larry's been hurt, pretty bad—you'll have to come get him. His horse fell with him. It's not very far."

Several of us grabbed our flashlights and went down the trail to where we saw Larry's horse, standing and grazing in the early dark, and we found Larry close by, lying on his back. He said, "I guess I'll have to have help to get back to the cabin. I don't think I can stand up and walk." We looked him over as well as we could with flashlights and couldn't find any blood. Larry said, "I don't think any bones are broken, but something's wrong with my shoulders." We couldn't make out what was wrong, but we sure didn't want to move him if his back was hurt. He moved himself around enough so we could see that at least he wasn't paralyzed. So four of us lifted him, two with hands under his shoulders and one on each leg, and carried him up to the cabin.

Jack asked him, "Can you manage any supper, Larry?" He tried, but couldn't raise his hands far enough, and every motion hurt, so Jack helped him eat, while the rest of us counseled about a doctor.

Doc Replogle of Lander, Charlie's brother, had been there only yesterday with Jim Gratiot, our boss at the Diamond G. It looked like he'd be the best bet. He and Gratiot had ridden out the day before, planning to spend the night at Rocky Mountain Lodge on Blackrock Creek. We could just hope that he'd still be there. If not, we'd just have to see what we could find out by phone from the lodge. Somebody was going to have to ride there through the night, about sixteen miles. We talked about drawing straws to pick who would ride. I said, "Aw, hell, I'll just take that big red pinto and do it. He sees better at night than I do in the daytime. Let's get at it."

I went out and put a halter on the big pinto and gave him a big feed of grain—he'd need it. He ate while I got into my warmest clothes—my wool socks and packs, Scotch cap, wool pants, heavy coat, and mittens, and my bat-wing chaps. It had gotten colder and was starting to spit snow, and I knew it might be a tough night.

Larry said his accident happened while they were riding in the dark up the steep trail to the cabin. The lodgepole pines grew close to the trail on both sides, and the thick roots crossed the trail like knotted ropes, making the going rough. At one point his horse shied at something and must have stumbled. He went down to his knees, and Larry jumped off, hanging on to the reins. Larry got his foot twisted in a root, he thought, and went down full-length. That was when something happened to his shoulders.

The pinto I'd picked wasn't the gentlest horse in the world, but he had the most trail savvy in our bunch. I'd ridden him before at night and knew his night sight was the best of any horse I'd ridden. I felt sure I was going to make it. Right after we started, and were inching our way down over those roots that caused Larry's trouble, the clouds parted and out came the moon. Lucky. I knew things would turn out right. As we rode down the trail, I could hear the bells as the boys pushed the bunch out on the parks on Soda Mountain.

About two miles out of camp, down by a cluster of soda springs we jumped a bunch of elk and something else making a snorting in the timber. As you fellows know, riding at night is no cinch, but somebody had to do it, and I'd stuck my neck out. We had it pretty easy till we got two miles or so from Turpin Meadows, when it started again to storm, with clouds and wind and spitting snow. But we were on the main trail by then, and the horse knew it, too. We heard owls hooting and some sounds of birds we'd disturbed. We got near some more elk and heard some cows barking to their calves, "Les' get out of here—there's trouble comin' down the trail."

When we got down the hill to the South Fork bridge, I was sure we had it made, for here was the old highway. We trotted across the bridge and past the dark buildings of Turpin Meadow Ranch—no lights anywhere, horse bells ringing off in the hills. We never stopped, just kept on going. As I remember, it was about eight miles uphill to Rocky Mountain Lodge. There was never much highway travel at night, none at all this night. I knew I had a good horse for distance—fat and strong. I wasn't exactly fresh, since I'd worked hard all day, first hunting and then packing in, besides all the miles I'd just ridden. But I was proud of that horse as we climbed the hill, and I knew we'd make it. We had no mishaps as we crossed the little wooded flat and rode up to the front door of the lodge.

I knew Cal Reed would be at his camp on the South Fork of Spread Creek. I also knew Mrs. Reed was a light sleeper, and I didn't want to get shot. There were some fist-sized rocks near the entrance so I picked one up and hammered on the front door, yelling all the while, "Hey! Mrs. Reed! Mrs. Reed! This is Joe Back! This is Joe Back! From the Sody Fork camp!" over and over. Larry was her son, but I didn't want to alarm her about him yet. I heard some mumbling inside, and somebody yelled, "Who are you out there?" So I called again, "This is Joe Back! From the Sody Fork! Is Doc Replogle still around?"

I heard the rattle of the lock, the door opened a crack, and a gun-barrel stuck out through it. I knew that had to be Sarah Reed herself. She was nobody's fool, and wasn't taking chances. She had to know who was there. "What's the matter, Joe?" she yelled through the closed door.

"It's Larry, Mrs. Reed. He fell off a horse and got kinda skinned up. He'll be all right, but knowin' the Doc might still be here, we thought it would be good if he could ride out and take a look at Larry in the morning."

When Mrs. Reed opened the door and said, "Come on in, Joe. I'll stir up the fire," I took a quick look to see that Pinto was all right, and went in as fast as I could. Mrs. Reed was all fluttery and excited, of course. She said, "We'll get Doc Replogle and take off right now!" Right now was about 2:30 in the morning and both Pinto and I had to have some rest. I did a little lying about Larry to calm her down. About then Jim Gratiot and Doc came out to see what the hullaballo was about. She had them bedded down in a room just off the main lodge room, and they had the door open, so they heard most of this. I sat down in a chair, all worn out. Mrs. Reed lit up some lamps, went out in the kitchen to put some coffee on, and brought out some doughnuts. She was somewhat pacified.

I explained to Jim Gratiot and Doc about Larry, said I didn't think he was too bad, but we all thought a doctor ought to look at him before we moved him. Just then Verne Meeks came in the door. He was a horse wrangler and his ears were sensitive to night uproar. He'd come to investigate. We wised him up, and he said, "I'll take your pinto down to the spring and water him. Then I'll take off his gear and turn him loose in the corral with plenty of hay and some oats. And, Joe, you look half dead. Better get some sleep." Sarah took the hint. She found a bedroll and a cot, and I just stretched out and went dead to the world.

It was too soon when voices woke me up. It was Mrs. Reed talking to Verne (a horse wrangler gets on the job before sunrise). She said, "Keep in my apaloosa, Parrot, and a horse for Doc. Better keep in a spare or two, we may need them. We'll start after breakfast. And, Verne, I'll leave you in charge while I'm gone."

A little more sleep and here came breakfast. I was pretty groggy but better than last night. At breakfast we had another volunteer—Einar Anderson. Einar had this stretch of highway for his job; it was a gravel road, not paved, and the department assigned upkeep jobs to different men for so many miles of road. Einar had a camp, four draft horses, a slip scraper, a fresno, and other gear, and we all knew him pretty well. He dropped in, heard the story, and said, "I think I'll go along. I've got my own horse and saddle. This is Sunday, and I'm not working today. You might need some help bringing Larry out."

We all started out soon after breakfast with Mrs. Reed on her pet, Parrot. We led a couple of spare horses and took the old Huey trail, a shortcut to the Buffalo, I hadn't used it at night because it was ciiffy, heavy timbered, and dangerous in the dark; but we didn't have any trouble in the daylight and reached the Soda Fork camp before eleven that morning. Everybody was in camp as none of the hunters wanted to go out till they saw whether a doctor was coming or not.

This was about fifty-five or sixty years ago. If my memory is still working, this is what happened. The boys took Pinto, gave him a good feed of oats, put hobbles on him, and turned him out with the horse bunch. The others were watered, tied up, and fed, ready to go back.

Doc Replogle, a very good doctor, gave Larry a careful examination. His diagnosis turned out to be that the collarbone had been pulled loose from his breastbone. Somehow, we had to get him in to the lodge. Could he possibly ride in?

Larry was game to try. They put his saddle on a very gentle horse. Doc strapped a pillow firmly to Larry's back to hold his shoulders up. Everybody who could help, did. Larry was boosted into the saddle. They hobbled the stirrups under the horse's belly with string and tied Larry's feet into the stirrups with heavy twine. Larry said he had strength enough in his hands to hold on to the horn. His mother led his horse behind Parrot. Einar went ahead to be sure the trail was OK, and Doc led the extra horse close behind for emergencies.

I saw the procession off and collapsed on my bedroll. I slept all that day and the next one I was still pretty groggy.

In the next few days all the hunters got their game, we filled all the licenses, and were going back to the ranch. We had to decide whether to pack out up the South Fork of the Buffalo to Cub Creek and go up it directly to the Diamond G, or to take the longer trail—up the Huey trail to the lodge, maybe stay the night there, and next day go over ToGwoTee Pass to the Diamond G. We all wanted to know how Larry was getting along, so we took the long way. Larry was there, able to get around some, but being pretty careful. Doc had decided he didn't need a hospital if he wouldn't work any more that season, particularly didn't lift anything and laid down whenever he felt like it.

Larry obeyed the Doc and wintered with his folks near Dubois. By spring, when the Diamond G opened up for dudes, he was back there at his job as horse wrangler and guide.

34

Don't Brag When You Get a New Set of Teeth

I'd been down to Lander and made my last payment on my new set of teeth. I was near Crowheart when I saw a man I knew digging a post-hole near the road, so I stopped to visit. My frind Lynn is a great jokesmith, and one joke he told was so funny I laughed till my teeth fell out into the dirt by the new posthole. We were both sitting on the running board of my old Model-T when this happened. The new teeth didn't fit too good, but I sure didn't want to lose them, so Lynn and I both scrambled awhile in the loose dirt, and finally Lynn found them. He carried them over to an irrigation ditch, washed them off, and handed them to me.

Lynn told me not to feel too bad. He wanted to tell me about new teeth he'd gotten last fall and what happened to his.

His ranch house was down in the bottomland, and he had climbed up to the field on top, where he was replacing some old rotten posts. He got tired and sat down to rest. The new teeth hurt, so he took them out and set them down on a rock beside him, while he puffed on a cigarette. This was in the late fall and it looked kind of stormy. Before he finished his cigarette, here came a hard wind and a blast of snow. Lynn grabbed his crowbar and shovel and headed for the house. By the time he missed his teeth, it was dark and snowing like hell. He put his tools in the tool shed and then pushed his way up the hill against a blizzard to get his teeth.

"I knew I was a damn fool to be up there in a blizzard, looking for a set of teeth in the dark, but I needed them and I was hungry. I gave up, though, and fought my way back to the house. Supper didn't go down so well, and my wife kidded me so much that I felt like a bigger damn fool than I really was. The next morning it was still storming—you remember, Joe, that was the earliest big winter storm in years. My wife and I went up to look for teeth, but the snowdrifts changed the look of the place so much that we were afraid we might just by accident step on the teeth and break them all to pieces.

"Before breakfast I watered my team and fed them hay and grain. My cattle were bawling, so I hooked up the team to the hayrack and went out to one of the stacks and fed a couple of loads, swearing at myself all the time. Those teeth cost plenty and I'd just bought a new car, and I was kinda shy on money. But anyway, when the storm got over we decided the only thing to do was to go down to Lander and get a new set. These worked pretty well, and I got along through the winter.

"When spring came, I was still faced with replacing that old rotten fence. Just like in the fall, I got tired and needed a smoke, so I sat down on a rock. I felt something funny in the region of my hip pocket. I felt around and came up with those lost teeth. That's the only time I've ever had my own teeth bite me on the rear end."

I almost laughed my teeth out again, but I held them in with my hand. I got back in the Model-T and headed for Dubois.

While I was driving up the road, I remembered another grinder story and what a jackpot another friend got himself into. This was at Rocky Mountain Lodge where I'd worked many seasons. Verne Meeks, Lester Lewis, and the boss were on horseback, rounding up horses down on Three-Mile Meadow. Cal, the boss, had the strongest voice I ever knew, one that any auctioneer from hades would be proud of. He had what he called his "rebel yell," the damnedest sound I ever heard issue from a human mouth. Some of the horses he was driving to the lodge turned to try to pass him, so he used his rebel yell on them. He forgot he was wearing a new set of teeth. He opened his mouth, and out came a sound that would scare any grizzly bear back into the timber. The horses turned, all right, and headed back up the hill with the rest of the bunch. The snow was about three or four inches deep by now, and Cal was on a high lope after the horse bunch, when he realized his teeth had come out with the rebel yell. He whirled his horse around and went back to look for those teeth. When Verne and Lester heard that horrible yell, they thought Cal had got into a jackpot and came looking for him. Cal cautioned·them not to ride around too much, because the horses might step on those teeth.

That snow didn't last long. While the boys were putting in a hunting camp in the Terrace Mountain country, Cal sneaked down into Three-Mile Meadow to look for his teeth. He was getting a lot of kidding. Lester reported that one time when he was riding down in Three-Mile Meadow he saw a badger going down a hole carrying a set of teeth that didn't belong to him.

Terrace Mountain
and the Bear Trees

errace Mountain is the Divide between South Fork of the Buffalo
and the Soda Fork. It's about eight miles long, north to south, and
has on it the greatest number of bear trees I've ever seen. I've seen
about seventy trees I've felt sure were killed by bear and I've seen four or
five bear actually doing this, one of them a grizzly.

The trees may be white-barked pine, lodgepole pine, or spruce. One
you suspect to be a bear tree is one that was discovered by a bear—usually
a black bear. It's usually a mature tree, full of sap and with heavy bark. A
bear will sit down and put his hind legs around a tree—sit there, grab the
lower parts of the bark, and rip the bark up, a foot or two at a time. He'll
sit and lick up the sap and all the insects attracted to it, with great enjoyment.
Sometimes he has such a good time that he will circle the trunk and pull
off all the bark for three or four feet up. That usually kills the tree. You
can tell this is the work of a bear by all the disturbed earth and tracks.

It was in the latter part of the thirties that I first saw a grizzly stripping
a tree—up on the northeast slopes of Terrace Mountain. We were camped
on the North Fork of the Buffalo, where Soda Fork runs into it, north of
Terrace Mountain. This was a fishing camp in the summer—maybe around
the last of July. Mrs. Hinckley, a lady from Virginia, and her son and I
were riding along the edge of timber, climbing the mountain, keeping out
of sight of the elk we knew were there. We had three quiet horses. I heard
some kind of a tearing sound ahead and held up my hand to get the other
two, riding behind me, to stop. We were in the shadow, and the big
grizzly ahead was in the sunlight, so we could plainly see what he was
doing. We'd been climbing hard, the horses were tired, and the wind
didn't give the bear away to them, so we were lucky. This big dirty-brown
grizzly, who weighed maybe a thousand pounds, was straddling the roots
of this big spruce, had pulled off the bark up to several feet up, and was

licking off sap and insects. He would stick out his long tongue, lick up sap, then pull off more bark with his claws and his mouth. He'd gone about half-way around the tree, when one of our horses heaved a big sigh, and that ended the picture. The bear, just now hugely enjoying himself, gave a big loud snort. There was what seemed like a small cyclone for about half a minute, as he went down the mountain and out of sight. We rode up to the tree to take in all the sights, while Mrs. Hinckley cursed herself for having left her camera in camp. This would have been an extraordinarily rare picture.

We continued on up the mountain, staying in the shade of the heavy timber, till we could see some elk ahead of us, lying in open grassy parks. We had to quiet down young Hinckley, who was an inveterate whistler, so we could see what we hoped to see. We were east of the elk, and the wind was from the west. We tied up our horses in the deep shade and sneaked along carefully to see what was going on. We found we'd happened on a baby-sitting pre-school presided over by a big black cow elk. This was many years ago, but it was a sight I shall treasure all my life, if I live to be a thousand.

There must have been thirty-five elk in sight, most of them young ones, running in circles, playing, butting each other, some lying down, some trying to nurse the big cow (she butted them away), all having great fun. You could see other cow elk back away from the youngsters, grazing, while the big black one took care of the nursery. The calves were not weaned yet, and only beginning to eat grass. Way off across the park, west of us, we could see what we thought were bull elk and spikes, lying down in the shade of the timber, chewing their cuds. We were lucky to have four or five minutes to take in this picture, when there came some kind of an uproar in the distance. The cows lifted their heads, barked to each other, got the bunch all gathered together, and ran off down the mountain.

I don't know if you've heard, or heard about, cow elk barking. I don't know myself if bulls do. The sharp bark of a cow is a warning that there is danger.

It was getting late by now, and we knew we had a long way to go, so we headed back down toward the North Fork and reached camp just before dark. My dear wife, Mary, who was cook, had supper ready for us.

For many years Terrace Mountain had been off limits to hunters to protect the elk nursery. But two years earlier hunter pressure had forced the Game Department to allow hunting here. We were extra lucky to have gotten there before the elk had been too sensitive and fearful of humans.

38

The Boss Had to Wrangle at Midnight

O ne fall day we were setting up a spike camp the boss had used for several years on Terrace Creek, or some called it Fremont County Line Creek. We dug a good spud-hole, put up the cook tent (with Shorty in charge as usual), a couple of wall tents for the hunters, a gear tent, and a couple of tepees for us guides. It was around October 1 and was warm and sunny.

We had a lot of horses to carry all the stuff—twenty-five or thirty head, and Cal had ordered us before we left the ranch to pasture the horse herd up on Terrace Mountain. We had two hunters with us, and Cal was bringing in the others.

Up on Terrace Mountain I'd seen more trees that had been killed by bear than I'd seen anywhere else. All of us knew that Terrace Mountain was great country for black bear and a few grizzlies. Besides me, the guides were Ray Boedeker, Verne Meeks, and Bill Neeman. We'd all hunted these mountains for several seasons, and we had reminded Cal about the bear, but he insisted we must throw the horses up on Terrace Mountain, so we did. After supper we put two horses on picket close to camp, put bells on about every eighth horse, and threw the bunch up on Terrace Mountain on fine feed, where we hoped they'd stay all night. We knew that if they got spooked during the night, they would have to come out past our camp, and on account of the bells we'd be well-warned. We all took turns at wrangling, two of us at a time. These years there were plenty of game around, so we had no trouble finding what the hunters needed.

We were wakened about midnight by jingle-jangle, jingle-jangle, jingle-jangle, the bells going by our camp, the horses heading for the main camp on the Buffalo. We knew what had happened—the horses had been spooked by bear.

Verne Meeks and I shared a tipi. We yelled to the others that we would get up, and saddle up, and wrangle. We crawled out of those warm bedrolls, pulled on our clothes, and stepped into the frosty cold night. We got our saddles, bridles, and blankets out of the gear tent. The picket horses didn't like those cold saddles being thrown on them. We rode down, wide of the horse bunch, got them turned, ran them back up past camp, and instead of Terrace, put them on the grassy parks up Nowlin Mountain, where we thought we wouldn't have any bear trouble that night. It took us about two hours to get that done.

We wrangled late that morning, because hunting season didn't open till the next day. I mean, Ray and Bill wrangled, while Verne and I took it easy, and the hunters kidded us. Cal, the boss, rode in about noon with the other three hunters we were expecting. He asked about the horses, and we told him about the trouble the night before and how we'd put them the second time on Nowlin Meadows. The boss said, "You didn't throw them high enough, boys. Tonight you take them up, way up, to the high parks on Terrace. If they come down, I'll wrangle them myself!"

We all got a laugh out of this. We told him, "You don't know, boss, what you're gettin' in for. Sure, we'll put 'em way high up on Terrace, but you're goin' to have a wranglin' job." He said, "OK, leave it to me. I'll take care of it."

It turned cold, snowed two or three inches in the afternoon. Sure enough, we threw the horse bunch way up high on Terrace Mountain, then we had supper and hit the sack early, because the five hunters and their guides were starting the hunt by daylight. I got up around midnight, felt the weight of snow on the tipi, and saw that it was clear now and the moon was shining.

The boss had thrown his bedroll in with the cook, so everything was in shape so far. About two o'clock we could hear the horse bells coming off the mountain and past our tents. Again jingle-jangle, jingle-jangle, jingle-jangle, past our camp and on down. We could hear the crunch, crunch of the horses' feet on the new snow. We could hear Cal's voice, "Hey, boys! Hey! Can't you hear!" He'd forgotten all about his promise to wrangle. Verne reached out of his bedroll and nudged me, "Joe, don't say a word!" Nobody else said a word, either. Cal yelled some more, "Hey, boys, Hey! Boys! I've hired the damnedest bunch of no-goods for guides and wranglers! Hey!" Nobody said a word. The hunters started muttering to themselves—they were wondering what was happening. Then all was quiet. We heard the last of the jingle-jangle as the last of the horses went on down the trail. I heard a gentle giggle from Verne but nothing more.

We all strained our ears to hear Cal tramping out to bring a picket horse to the gear tent. We heard him blow on the bit to get the frost out, then bridle the horse, then heard him brush the snow off Randy's back and throw on the blanket and saddle, all the while swearing at the goddam guides you hire these days. We could hear him buckle up his old hairy batwing chaps, then drag on the reins as he stepped on, cussing Randy meanwhile, "You behave now, you goddam fool, try any tricks with me an I'll jab these spurs into ya a foot deep."

As he trotted his horse down the trail we knew what he was up against, and felt kind of sorry for him, but he'd made his brag and was stuck with it, so after a few laughs we went back to sleep.

As I remember the trail, it led downhill through heavy timber into the big grassy parks on the Buffalo Fork, before you could get around the horse bunch and head them back. It was close to daylight when the other horse on picket began whinnying and jumping around and raising hell, waking us all up. We all knew it meant Cal was coming up the trail with the horse bunch, so we climbed out of our bedrolls and got our clothes on, ready to help him get them all into the corral. About then we heard the jingle-jangle of the bells. After we'd helped get the corralling done, Cal stepped off his horse, not saying a word. We knew he was as mad as any of us would have been. I took Randy's reins, unsaddled him, put the gear away, and rubbed him down good. He'd had quite a job. I didn't water him then, not till he'd cooled down some. Cal had been lucky to have moonlight. It started clouding up after we'd corralled the horses. We just got the pole up when it started spitting snow.

Shorty hollered out of the cook tent, "Come 'n' get it or I'll throw it out!" As we straggled toward the cook tent, Verne says to Cal, "Hey, boss, when we turn the horses out tonight, shall we put them up on Terrace Mountain?"

Cal was struggling out of the old black chaps as he answered, scowling, "You can put them horses anywhere you damn please. You can put 'em up Pike's Peak if you want to."

That was the last time we put them on Terrace, so the rest of the trip we had no horse trouble. There were plenty of elk, the hunters were lucky, and Cal got over his mad.

Horse With No Hair on His Tail

We were camped (hunting camp) in mid-September on Grouse Creek under Grouse Mountain. There were just two guides, Larry Reed and me, one hunter, and a good cook. Larry and I both wrangled horses. Larry's hunter killed a big bull moose not far from Railroad Ridge, higher up the South Fork of Spread Creek so Larry and I saddled up three horses to ride and picked out a couple of pack horses. We had some trouble with one of the pack horses. His name was Medley Wertz, named for the man the boss bought him from.

Medley was a big strong horse, and once you got him packed, you usually couldn't ask for a better one. He was an irascible sort, sometimes as gentle as a cat, but sometimes he was a wildcat. This time we blindfolded him, then tied a bowline around his shoulders so we could pull up a hind foot. He was ten or twelve years old by now, and we'd handled him for three or four years so were well acquainted with him. We thought we'd get him broken in for the season before the main bunch of hunters came along. He was a strange sort of horse. Sometimes he thought he was an elephant, and sometimes he was sure he was a weak little cat. We had to throw him sometimes to put a packsaddle on him. I've seen the time when I had to put a pack on him while he was hog-tied and lying down, and that's some job. This time we were watching for his cow-kick. You could be standing by his shoulders, and he could raise a hind foot and kick you on the chin without any trouble at all.

We got the blanket and packsaddle on him, and plenty of sling-rope round on the saddle to take care of the big moose quarters. We already had a big gentle horse named Billy saddled, and we thought we were ready to go. We let Medley's hind foot down and tailed him to the other horse before we took the blindfold off.

Larry and his hunter were planning to go deer hunting after we got the moose packed on the two horses. I would bring the pack horses and moose quarters back. Shorty gave each of us a package of lunch, which we wrapped in our coats and tied behind the cantles. I told Shorty we'd be back in the afternoon, or before dark, I hoped.

We took off, Larry ahead with his hunter, me behind, leading the two pack horses. We went up the Spread Creek Trail toward Railroad Ridge to locate the moose. Larry took us right to it. He'd dressed it out, quartered it, brushed it up, and dragged the entrails off to one side. We knew we were close before we got there, for the ravens, jays, and Clark's crows were telling us all about it as they fought over the entrails.

This was some fifty years ago but as I remember it, we knew Medley Wertz was the only horse we'd have trouble with and tied him up near the saddle horses. The other horse, Billy, was very reliable and gentle. We thought we'd put the front quarters and the head on him and the hind quarters on Medley. Larry's hunter was holding the halter rope. Larry cautioned him, "Now, if he jumps, turn his head away from me and toward Joe. Joe's on the left side, and that's the most dangerous side."

We had no trouble at all with Billy, except it's slow and heavy work, getting the front quarters upon the saddle and cinched down tight with the sling ropes. We put the moose's head, nose up, on top of the load, with the horns (and they were nice horns) down along the sides and held them down with sling-ropes and half-hitches, so they wouldn't slip in case of trouble. We took Billy off to one side and tied him to a tree.

Now for Medley. We untied him and led him up. When he smelled the blood, he snorted and jumped and flounced around. Larry wiped his hands full of moose blood and then wiped them over Medley's nose, so that's all he could smell and he quieted down. We blindfolded him again, tied a hind leg up, and tied him solidly to a stout tree, with the hunter holding on the rope in case he broke loose.

Larry lifted one of the hind quarters of moose—a lot of weight, but Larry was husky and strong. I helped him with the sling-ropes, and we got that piece of meat tied on hard and fast. Medley had given us no trouble so far. Larry got in a word to me, "You have to watch this hunter. The damn fool is scared of horses and probably won't do what we tell him, but we'll have to trust him." While I was hoisting up the other quarter and Larry was ready to get the sling-rope in place from his side, it happened. The horse lunged, jumped my way, and knocked me over as I was lifting that 200-pound hind quarter. I went down on my back on a rock, with that quarter on my chest. What saved me was plenty of tall rye grass and brush that somewhat cushioned my fall. It knocked me out.

44

What brought me to was that hunter laughing. He thought it was a joke. Larry says to him, "Hey! You damn fool! It's no joke! We mighta killed him! Maybe we did!" I came out of it swearing at the dude, at the moose, at the whole damn world. My back hurt bad, but somehow I knew I hadn't broken any bones. I staggered up to my feet, and Larry says, "Joe, you all right? You sure you're all right?" I staggered around and felt myself all over. I said, "I guess so, but I bet I'll be sore tomorrow." Between us, we hoisted up that other quarter and roped it solidly into place. Medley caused no trouble this time. I walked around in a circle, moved my shoulders, had Larry feel me all over and rub my sore back. We made pretty sure that I was OK.

Larry untied the other horse and led him over close to Medley Wertz. Medley was still blindfolded and with one hind leg tied up. The gentle horse had a long tail. Just below the bone of the tail we tied Medley to it with three strong half-hitches. Then we loosened the rope over Medley's back and let his hind foot down. We took off his blindfold and watched to see what he would do.

Medley had been packed plenty of times before, but he still thought he knew some tricks that hadn't been tried. This time he turned his head and found he was tied plenty tight to Billy. Then he gathered his legs under him, and halfway tried to buck his load off. When it didn't work, he quieted and stood there. A lot of rolling snorts came out of his nose, and he glared at us but that was all. I thought maybe we'd cooled him off.

I untied my saddle horse and mounted him, rode over to Billy and untied him, then rode around in a circle a couple of times, leading both horses, to see what Medley would do. He didn't try anything, just led like a well-trained pack horse. Larry says to me, "Think you'll be OK, Joe? When you get to camp, you can get Shorty to help you unload. Maybe you'll have to blindfold Medley and tie up a hind foot again. You sure you feel all right?" I said, not very enthusiastic, "OK, we'll make it all right." We said goodbye and I took off the same way we'd come, over an old game trail.

This trail wasn't maintained, just used by game, and a couple of small logs had fallen over it, close together. These deadfalls didn't cause us any trouble coming in, and now, going out, riding real slow, the saddle horse and the first pack horse handled the logs all right. I was turned around in my saddle, watching. The first pack horse had cleared the logs. I thanked God we had both pack horses freshly shod.

I thought Medley was doing all right. He crossed the first log. Then he saw his chance to make trouble, and he took it. He braced his front feet

and leaned back, pulling with all his might. He was a big horse, maybe twelve- to thirteen-hundred pounds, and those two quarters of moose gave him more weight to pull with. I backed my horse up, and Billy backed, too. Tailing up a horse can be a painful thing. I've tailed up a lot of pack horses in my time, and this is the only time I had real trouble. I gave my horse all the slack I could, and so did the other horse, but that damn fool Medley, snorting, was planning to make all the trouble he could. It looked like he was just planning to make it as interesting as he could, to vary the monotony. I cussed him with all the words I knew, and I knew plenty, but they didn't do any good. Wouldn't you know, this time of all times, all three half-hitches on the tail pulled off, taking most of the hair off that tail. And wouldn't you know, after that, he *didn't* turn and take off through the timber, bucking and snorting, he just stood there! Looking like he was saying, "Now, what are you going to do next, you damn fool?"

I got off my horse and tied him to a lodgepole pine and went past Billy, who was shaking his head and moaning—he must have been hurting terrible. Just as I went by his tail, he shook it and drops of blood flew all over me. Medley just stood there while I picked up his halter rope and followed me, gentle as a lamb. I walked on just a little ways to the main trail, where I tied him to a five- or six-inch lodgepole pine and proceeded to do what I had to do to that bastard. I put a blindfold back on him, tied both front legs together, and tied up a hind foot again. I led Billy over to Medley, and half-hitched him to Medley's tail, making the hitch just as strong as I could, even while I was thinking, "You bastard, it would only serve you right if Billy pulled *your* tail off."

Next I checked over Medley's pack—the lash-rope and the sling-rope on both sides of his load. It all seemed tight. Then it was Billy's turn—he had the heavier load, front quarters and head, and the ropes were still all tight. I went over my saddle horse and tightened up the cinch. Then I checked myself. I'd kind of come apart with all the cussing, and until that minute I'd forgotten about what Medley did to me, back where we'd loaded. I was sore and shaky, but I was sure I could make camp. I grieved at the blood spattered all over Billy's hind end, decided there wasn't anything more I could do to help him at this point and that the only thing to do was to get back to camp. I untied Medley's front legs, let his hind foot down, and took off his blindfold. He was just as quiet and gentle as you could ask for, not even snorting. I untied him from the tree and jerked him around some, because I was mad at him for the way he'd treated me after I'd been plenty good to him. I untied my horse and got on him,

Medley's lead rope dallied around my horn, and we went off down the trail together. Camp was about a mile and a half away.

As we rode along, I was looking forward to Shorty's help in unpacking. He was older than me, but pretty strong. I'd be in luck that way. I wasn't so sure about Medley as he could make plenty of trouble. But he didn't. He followed along, gentle as a lamb, all the way to camp. Just before we got there, I could hear people talking. It was mid-afternoon by then, and I realized the two other guides with their hunters had come in from the lodge and were in the cook tent talking with Shorty—I'd have more help.

They heard us coming, and all came out. They took in the whole business right off. Jim and Harley, the guides, knew Medley—they'd used him before. We had a couple of meat poles already in place from other seasons. We led Billy under them and got ropes to hoist first the big moose head and horns, then the two front quarters off his load. They took off his pack saddle and gear, while I rummaged into our camp supply for a kind of salve we'd found useful lots of times—bear grease mixed with sulfa powder. We smeared it all over Billy's tail. He didn't like it much and I felt for him. He moved around a good deal, but he didn't fight. There were quite a few flies that had found him, but they left when we put on the salve. I gave him a good feed of oats and led him over to the spring for a big drink of water. Then we turned him loose to go with the rest of the bunch up to the Grouse Creek meadows.

We came to Medley last. He didn't deserve anything better. I led him under the meat pole and went through the handcuff routine again— blindfold, tie front feet together, lift hind foot with a bowline over his shoulders. Then the fellows untied his pack and hoisted the hind quarters to the pole. I undid the handcuffs and unsaddled the bastard. I hobbled him, said, "No oats for you this time, you son of a bitch," and turned him loose. He knew all about hobbles, made his way to the spring and got a drink, then followed the other horses up to the meadows.

We didn't use Billy the rest of that season. He stayed with the horse bunch and fattened up on the grass of the mountain meadows. His tail healed up and before the end of the season showed some signs of hair. I didn't work for that outfit next season, so I didn't find out how Billy was next year. I wish I knew. I wish I could do it all over again.

The Rancher
Who Hated Nature

Before I run out of Tom Benton's big pile of words, I want to get in a few about this rancher who hated nature. Now, my friends, I'm no angel. And, looking back, I see things I've done that I should be ashamed of. I had a small ranch once, and a neighbor asked me one day to help him round up some horses. We located five or six of his horses and threw them down toward the ranch. It was about noon, so we tied our horses to trees and sat down on a log to eat the lunches we carried.

As we ate, we could see a big anthill on a flat sandy place. The ants were busy adding details to their beautiful castle. I was admiring them. I said to my neighbor, "I gotta think a lot of them ants. They must be great designers, as well as hard workers, to build such a castle, protecting them from weather and cold and wet, full of corridors and rooms." We got our lunch eaten, went over to the spring and got a drink of water, and started to untie our horses to drive the rest of the bunch down to the ranch. I was leading my horse over to the spring to fill up, when much to my surprise I saw Jim go over to the anthill and start kicking sand and ants around. "I hate ants!" he said. "I'll show these little beggars they ain't so hot." While from my seat in the saddle I was marvelling at his actions, he said (untying his horse and getting on), "Les go!" without even giving his thirsty horse a drink of water.

There weren't any words in Tom Benton's pile to describe how I felt as we rode on down the hills. Two or three months later I had another demonstration from this neighbor.

We were together, discussing a ditch that watered both our places, when we saw a little badger, about half-grown, come trotting down the ditch bank. He went into a culvert near us, where the ditch crossed the road. Jim had two dogs with him, a collie and an airedale. They were about fifty feet off. They thought they had a rabbit treed under a pile of sagebrush and were busy doing their stuff when the badger came along the ditch bank. I thought Jim's dogs generally looked about half-starved.

I didn't say anything to Jim about the badger, but Jim had seen him, too, and called the dogs over to each end of the culvert and sicced them on the badger. These dogs knew more about badgers than their owner did. They didn't even want to came close to the culvert as they knew what would happen. Jim kept siccing them on, till the Airedale finally crawled into the culvert, where the badger grabbed a paw and nearly had it gnawed off before he could crawl back to safety. I'd had enough of this and told Jim I had stuff to do across the river, and I'd see him later. But he said, "I'd like you to stay while I run down to the house a minute. I want to talk something over." So I waited with the dogs. I could see no way I could defend this ferocious little warrior without making Jim my enemy, so I sat down on a rock and rolled a smoke till Jim came back. Jim came on a little trot. He had a big six-shooter in one hand and a grin on his face. He said, "I'll show that little beggar." Jim bent down, shoved a dog out of the way, and shot that little gladiator four or five times as he was coming gamely at Jim. He died right there in the end of the culvert, still full of fight.

Jim walked over and picked up the bloody little fighter by the tail, carried him to the edge of the river and threw him in, "There!" he said, "I showed him!"

I had enough of this. I asked Jim, "What would you have done if the badger had a gun?" He said, "Aw, hell, don't be a damned fool!"

Badger

I was digging out an irrigation ditch to water a piece of land I had cleared on the ranch I owned on Wind River. I had a good team and plow, and I was scooping out dirt with a little two-horse fresno, which worked very fine. The ditch was about four feet wide. I'd been working on it about a month or so and thought I was getting a good job done. It was a warm day in June. The horses needed a rest, so I let them have it, while I sat on the bank and rolled a Bull Durham.

There were quite a few badgers in that country. I never bothered them and they never bothered me, but that day they treated me to a sight I never believed could happen. Forty feet down the ditch was a male badger, spinning around in a circle, looking all the time at a hole up the bank.

There was no wind and the horses were quiet. I pinched out my cigarette and squirmed around to where I could get a better view. I looked hard at the hole up above the badger in the bank, and I could see another badger, looking out. I took it to be a female, watching the male badger's gymnastics. I thought this must be courting time among the badgers. As he spun around, the male badger kept watching to see if the female appreciated his antics. Every once in awhile he'd stand on his hind feet as he danced. When she had her head stuck way out from the bank, and he was sure she was watching, he'd stand on his *front* paws and raise his hind feet into the air. He went through the whole show several times. This was my first badger theatre, and I sure enjoyed it. Then one of the horses snorted some flies away, and the actors disappeared in a hurry.

It was noon by then, so I took the team back to the barn and fed and watered them. I went up to the house, where Mary had dinner ready, and told her my yarn. She said, "You're probably the biggest liar in Wyoming, but I'll pretend to believe it."

After this, I was very careful what nature lover I told this to, knowing that probably no one else would believe it, either.

Bobcat

Early one bright spring morning, my wife, Mary, and I were wakened by our dog Monkey barking. We were up late the night before at a party in Dubois, and we weren't overjoyed by his noise. What we saw made us glad we had wakened.

Monkey was black with white and brown accents, a fine stock dog and a good protector. He was about twenty-five feet from the biggest bobcat we'd ever seen and maybe twenty feet from the bedroom window. The cat wasn't even looking at the dog. He was sitting on his short tail and scratching at a banged-up ear—he must have been in a fight. Monkey was telling him all about it, what he would do if he had a mind to, but he didn't move any closer. The bobcat was nearly as big as that border collie. He gave us one glance, showing that he saw us at the window, stood up and trotted off toward Mary's garden, never honoring the dog with one look. That bobcat had been places and seen things. Monkey saw us, too, and barked more furiously, following the cat without getting any closer.

We moved to another window, watching that richly furred animal, tawny with black flecks, walk with the darnedest swagger I ever saw, then sit down on his tail in the edge of the garden and scratch gently again at the battered ear. He straightened up and cooly walked into the underbrush and disappeared. Monkey put on the darnedest smirk you ever saw, practically saying out loud, "I showed that big so-and-so who's boss around here!"

The next day I was driving out toward the highway on our road, when I met our neighbor, Jim, in his car. He motioned for me to stop—he wanted to talk. I told him about this magnificent cat and how we admired him. Jim said, "Why didn't you shoot the damn thing?"

I said, "Why, this time of year the fur's no good, and he hadn't done me any harm. He was beautiful, fat and sassy, and looked like he's making a good living. Why shoot him?"

Jim said, "He was sure making a good living all right. Two nights ago he got into my chickenhouse and killed five or six of my hens and two roosters. From the sign I could see, it was a bobcat. I'da shot him!"

"Maybe I'da done different if I'd knowed that or if it was my chickens."

Jim said, "Oh, go to hell with a damn fool like you," and speeded up past me.

That summer Jim sold his ranch, moved away, and I never saw him again. I was glad to be rid of that nature lover.

Ranger Trails and Game Trails

Mary and I kind of overspent ourselves one fall. We bought a ranch we were building up for a dude ranch. We bought lumber, windows, roofing, nails, and stuff, and I cut logs to build several dude cabins. This place wasn't irrigated yet and didn't raise any hay so I had to arrange to pasture my horse bunch (about eighteen head) with someone else for the winter. We were just plain short of cash. I wasn't planning to guide that fall, but a fellow I knew from the Turpin Meadow country came along just before hunting season. The going wages for a guide those days was about $6.00 a day. This man offered me $2.00 a day more if I'd run a camp for him. I knew I wasn't the best qualified man to run a camp, but, hell, I was really pinched for cash, so I took him up on it.

A week or so before the season opened, I drove over the pass and down to this bird's place. I thought I'd be shoeing horses to start with (he had about forty head), and I wasn't bad at that job. But the boss and a couple of other guys had got it done earlier.

The outfitter already had his main camp all set up on the South Fork of the Buffalo. The one he had in mind for me would be on Leidy Creek, about halfway between Spread Creek and Leidy Lake. He already had his permit for the site, so that was OK.

Claire Shippen and I got the camp set up three or four days before the season opened. We cut come corral poles from lodgepole pine and built the corral. There were tents for the hunters and tipis for the guides, a tent for gear, and a big cook tent with its spud-hole dug. The main supplies were stacked. We even packed in eight-foot boards for the spudhole and so we could make a table and seats, using lodgepole Xs for legs.

Claire was a guide I knew and liked and had guided with before. Now, all we needed were hunters and more guides and a cook.

54

We had about six or seven pack horses, and of course we had come in on saddle horses, driving the pack animals ahead of us. About four or five inches of snow had fallen, but most of it had melted, and the weather was fine. It looked like our first two-week hunt would be off to a good start.

I was wondering about Billy Stillson's camp as competition with mine. I knew him from other years—he'd been bringing a doctor into this area to hunt for several seasons back. His camp had a cook, a guide, Billy himself, and a hunter. I was delighted when Claire brought word that Billy had showed up to tell them at the lodge that he was taking the doctor to the South Fork of the Buffalo to look into the rumor about a big grizzly. It looked like there wouldn't be any camp besides ours in this area.

The next afternoon here came the boss with four hunters, two men he said were guides he'd just hired, and a cook. One guide was a great big man from Cheyenne. The other guide, I found out, was a cowboy from the grass country near Sheridan. He was eight or ten years older than me, and a real hand with horses, but he hadn't been in the mountains much. The four hunters were oil men from Oklahoma and I soon found out they were never very far from the bottle.

The guides were O'Leary from Cheyenne and Johnson, the cowboy. The cook was Bill Thompson. The boss introduced us all the way round. Then he said it would be long after dark before he got home, and he left right away. The hunters got their stuff arranged in their tents, and the guides got organized, too. Claire Shippen shook his head at me, "Joe," says he, "I wonder what we're in for, this trip." I wondered, too.

We found that Bill Thompson, the cook, was an early riser, which suited us just fine. The hunters told us right away that they *didn't* like to get up early. Claire and I tried to make it clear that late starters didn't have very good luck hunting elk, and they gave in—sort of. They said, "OK, you're the guides, have it your way." So the first day of the hunt, the cook and Claire and I roused up everybody. We picked out horses that we thought would suit each hunter, as we sized them up, and got the hunters to try them out. We guides all got the stirrups adjusted and tried to make sure the hunters knew they were to tie up the horses by the halter ropes and not the bridle reins. We had breakfast, and Bill put up good lunches for everybody. We found out right away that O'Leary, the man from Cheyenne, didn't volunteer to do anything. He just stayed in the tent and talked to the dudes, unless I told him to do something. Claire and I decided that he was high on conversation and short on performance, and we knew he would have to have the biggest, strongest, and gentlest horse in the bunch.

Since none of the hunters and only two of the guides had been in this valley before, Claire and I made a point of describing the lay of the land. We pointed out the prominent peaks as landmarks, showed the directions of the creeks, told where you could expect to find elk and other game. I assigned a guide to each hunter and directed each off to a different drainage, to try their luck today. Claire and I each had our own hunter, and the two were impatiently waiting to get going, while we did all this.

Before we started, I checked every hunter's rifle. They all had good scabbards tied to their saddles, and I made it clear they must have no shells in their chambers, but plenty in the magazines.

The big man from Cheyenne, with his hunter, went down Leidy Creek, intending to cross Spread Creek and hunt in the Grouse Mountain country upstream from the crossing—real prime hunting country. Johnson, his hunter and I started down the same way. They were to cross Spread Creek and hunt downstream.

Our impatient hunters had to wait while I talked with Bill, the cook, about the horses. He was afoot, of course, I asked him to leave them in the corral for an hour or so, then turn them into the big meadow nearby where they'd spent the night. Claire and I hobbled the horses we knew would be homesick, had bells on the ones we thought needed them, and we had two on picket on good feed. It surprised and pleased us to find out that Bill had been around horses more than we had a right to expect. We could hear elk bugling, and we were really in a hurry by now.

Claire said he wanted to go upstream past Leidy Lake, where Leidy Creek headed, and then hunt up Carmichael Fork. He'd had good luck up that way other seasons. I said OK, I'd start the same way and head off to the right. We parted company about a mile or so up the trail and didn't see each other again till afternoon.

I couldn't do anything more for any of the other hunters, so I put my attention to mine. We traveled around through a succession of parks and timber. After about an hour we heard two shots, close together, so maybe Claire and his hunter had connected, we hoped. We saw several bunches of elk, but no big bull, and a moose below us in a bunch of willows. The hunter said he would wait for a big bull. When noon came, we tied our horses to trees by their halter ropes and got out our lunches. We both made sure our rifles were out of their scabbards and within easy reach. After lunch we stretched out and took a nap. This is just about what the elk do. They go in little groups into heavy timber, lie down, chew their cuds, and listen for any danger.

About 2:30 or 3 o'clock we heard some sound of movement in the

56

timber. We thought we should try stalking elk. We put our guns back in their scabbards, tied our coats back on the saddles, and moved carefully ahead, leading our horses. We hadn't gone 100 yards when I heard a low whistle and looked behind me to see my hunter taking his gun out of its scabbard. He took careful aim at something I couldn't see and shot twice. He said to me, "Hell, that was a big fat mule deer with the prettiest horns I ever saw. He was drinking from a spring right down there and raised his head up and looked around, just posing. And I missed him both shots!" I found out later he really was an expert shot, and no wonder he was mad at himself. We went to the spring, saw deer tracks, but no blood. We followed his trail, made some circles, and convinced ourselves that the shots really were clean misses. By now it was late in the afternoon, and I figured we were at least three miles from camp and that we'd better head back. Neither of us heard any more shots. We wondered if anyone had connected. We gave our horses good drinks at the spring and started for camp.

On the way, we were passing a small hill when we both heard something. The hunter was just behind me, and we both pulled up our horses. There was a little two-year-old shiny-haired cow moose with her head down, going down the hill, and going up, facing her, waddled a big porcupine, with all his quills straight up. He was squealing a little, mad about something or other. The moose started *backing up* the hill, careful to keep her nose out of reach of the porcupine. Neither of them noticed us. About then the moose heard us. She whirled around and raced up the hill as fast as she could go. The porcupine never changed pace. He proceeded uphill, squealing to himself. The hunter said, "I've seen a lot of things in my time, Joe, but never anything like that." "Neither have I," I answered. "I noticed the moose didn't have any quills in her nose. She had savvy."

Just before dark we reached the hunting camp. The cook was clattering pots and pans. I could see a horse in the corral, and the bars were up. The hunter had unsaddled his own horse, and turned him into the corral. O'Leary's big husky horse was tied on the outside of the corral by his bridle reins, with his saddle and other gear untouched, and I could hear O'Leary muttering inside his tent. (He had a tent to himself.) I had an inkling then of what we had ahead of us.

I took my hunter's horse into the corral, unsaddled him, took all the gear into the gear tent, gave the horses a good feed of oats, and got ready to bring in the bunch. I could hear bells not far off, so I knew they hadn't strayed. I was just up the hill when Claire and his hunter showed up. Claire said, "Just a minute, Joe, and I'll help you." We gathered up the

58

horses, got them all into the corral, and grained them all. I unsaddled O'Leary's horse, stood his rifle up against a tree, and put his gear away, wondering to myself what happened to our cowboy and his hunter. Just then they came in. The cowboy, Charley Johnson, showed he knew about horses, all right. He took care of both his horses, putting all the gear where it belonged, leading them to the stream for a drink, and grained them outside the corral, where the other horses couldn't interfere.

At the ranch, as always, the cook packed plenty of meat for the first few days, because you can't count on game right away, and Bill Thompson was showing proudly what he could do with it. We had piping hot steak with beans and potatoes and lots of good baking powder biscuits with butter, jam and fruit. Everybody was hungry and dove into it.

Jack O'Leary was up at the head of the table, telling the ones near him what football players he and his brother were in college. When I could get a word in edgewise I asked him, "How come you didn't take care of your horse when you came in?" He answered, "Hell, man, I'm a big game guide, not a horse wrangler!" At that, his hunter, down at my end of the table, gave a loud snort and fell to laughing. What's this all about? I wondered. The table was all of a sudden quiet. Everybody was watching O'Leary, who was stuffing himself with meat and potatoes. Claire broke the silence with welcome news. "Hey!" he said, "Me and my hunter got us a fine fat bull up on Carmichael Fork this mornin'. It's all ready to pack in tomorrow or next day." Everybody congratulated the two, and started trading the day's experiences. Bill Thompson was aware of the cloud hanging over his table and started noisily around with the coffee pot, filling up the tin cups.

The first one to get up and say he was going to hit the hay was Jack O'Leary. I though "Good, we got rid of him!" The rest of the bunch all helped clear away the dishes, dumping them by the handful into the hot water in the big pan. Claire said to me, "Les wrangle them horses, Joe." I said, "First, we gotta pick a couple of good ones to put on picket." So we got at it. As we left the tent, the hunters were telling Bill what a swell cook he was, and he was nodding and grinning, very pleased. We went on down to the corral and Charlie Johnson joined us. We saddled up the horses we were going to picket. The bunch was all grained up and ready to go. We took them up on the mountain meadows they were used to by now.

It was a lot colder, now. After we got our three horses on picket, and the gear put away, we could hear crackling sounds coming from the hunters' tents. We knew they were starting fires to warm up. The lantern glow was shining through the tents' canvases.

Seeing the light in the tent where O'Leary's hunter was, I walked up there and called, "Is it OK to come in?" He said "OK, come on in" He was about ready to crawl into his sleeping bag, but we sat on his cot and talked for awhile. "How did you and O'Leary get along today?" I asked him. He gave a snort. "If that guy's a big game guide I'm a Holy Roller minister. Right soon after we left camp we came on fresh elk sign and followed the tracks a ways. I says, 'We better stalk 'em, huh? He says, 'We gotta get back to the ranger trail.' 'Ranger trail?' I asks. 'Yes,' he says, 'trees marked with a nick 'n' a slash. No trails off that way except game trails.' That's what we did all day. Right from the ranger trail we caught some glimpses of elk, but O'Leary wouldn't leave the trail to get closer. We did get a good look at a cow moose and calf. There's game around, all right, but that guy's just afraid he'll get lost. If you assign him to me any more, I might just as well go back to the ranch and go home."

I replied, "We'll sure do something about that. Claire Shippen's hunter got his elk. I'll see if he'll be willing to see what he can do with O'Leary. That be all right with you?" He said, "That's fine. That's OK. Be a good trade."

When I reached our tipi, Claire was crawling into his sleeping bag. I told him what was up, and he said he thought the trade in hunters would be all right. "My hunter feels pretty happy about that elk. He said he was kinda tired and might want to stay in camp tomorrow. Maybe he wouldn't mind at all goin' out with O'Leary and sizin' him up. We can go pack in his elk day after tomorrow if it turns out that way."

"You left the quarters brushed up good?"

"Yes, and hung the head up pretty high in a tree. We left a lot of human scent around, coyotes and such won't bother for awhile, and it's lot colder up there than it is here. I'd like to show O'Leary's hunter a good day's hunting. I could sure see at supper he wasn't happy."

Bill Thompson, the cook, roused us up before daylight. He was starting up the fire and banging pots and pans around when Claire, Cowboy Charley, and I saddled up our picket horses and went off to wrangle. There was no trouble with the horses, and we brought them in just in time to hear Bill holler, "Come an' get it!" It was almost sunrise. We grained the herd and made sure they were all in good shape before we went up the hill to breakfast.

All we could hear from the "big game guide's" tipi were a lot of loud snores. I didn't bother him. We three joined the others at breakfast. They

60

were talking over what they might do today, and I told them the whole situation. Claire's hunter said that would be fine with him. He would take a rest after breakfast and see O'Leary when he saw fit to get up. He still had a deer license to fill, and he could see from yesterday's tracks that plenty of deer were around.

I asked Bill after breakfast to pick out a horse that hadn't been used yesterday, saddle him up to wrangle, and then feed and water him and put him on picket for the day. Bill was tickled. He said, "I ain't been on a horse for awhile, and I'd like to do the wranglin'." Then we all went down to the corral and picked out fresh horses for everybody. I noticed that the horse O'Leary had ridden showed the beginning of cinch and kidney sores. I warned everybody to just leave him alone till those healed. Then we picked another big, strong, gentle horse for O'Leary and put extra padding under the saddle.

My hunter and I took off for the same drainage we hunted in yesterday. We ate lunch and lay down for a short while, when we heard some sounds of movement near us and decided we should stalk some elk afoot. We carried our rifles and left the horses tied up. We had just left the little park, crossed a bit of timber, and came into another open, when a nice bull elk came right out in of us from the left. Wham! The hunter shot once and got him in the heart. He dropped right there, which is unusual; I've see heart-shot elk run a hundred yards before dropping.

We got right at dressing him out. My hunter knew what he was about. He helped me drag the entrails away from the meat, rustling up dry branches and put the quarters on top of them, hair side up, while I was doing the slow job of skinning out the cape for a mount. He then gathered the green branches to pile on top to keep the birds off.

We went back for the horses. The hunter put his gun in his scabbard, said, "Hey! My camera's in my saddle bag, let's go back for a picture!" And what do you know, there on the entrails was a mother black bear and two cubs! The hunter got a good photo before she chased the cubs off out of sight. "A photo's better than a dead mother bear!" said my hunter, happy. I said, "OK, let's go back to camp. But let's take care of that good liver, first." I was glad for the piece of canvas I had tied on behind my cantle. It was the right size to wrap the liver in to carry it home, tied on to the same place on the back of the cantle.

It was only two or three miles back to camp. Bill was the only one there. He said the "big game guide" got up a little before noon and was kind of peeved that I'd switched hunters on him, but he calmed down after a bit. They decided they'd follow my advice and hunt up toward Grouse Mountain again.

We three had a cup of coffee, and the hunter went to his tent. It was starting to get dark by now. We had watered our horses good along the last stretch of trail. I unsaddled them and turned them into the corral, brought in the picket horse and saddled him, put the extra gear away, and took off up the mountain to wrangle. I could hear bells, so I knew we had *some* horses anyway. Just as I left, I heard sounds on the trail and saw O'Leary, with his hunter riding behind him, coming up the trail. I just waved and went on, but I stopped before I was out of sight to look back. Just like last night, the "big game guide," paying no heed to his hunter, tied his horse by the bridle reins to the corral and walked toward his tent. I went on, found all the horses and brought them in. O'Leary's hunter had the bars down and ran to help me wing in the bunch. I had let them all drink up at the creek on the way in, so all that was left to do was grain them and select a picket horse and take care of him. Cowboy Charley and Claire had come in already and taken care of their horses.

It was almost dark. We just had time to exchange a few words by the corral when Bill yelled out, "Come an' get it or I'll throw it out!" We headed for the cook tent.

At supper, I asked O'Leary's hunter how they did. O'Leary said, "We done it this time, didn't we?" grinning at his hunter. "Yeah," said the hunter, "it did work out all right." He went on, "It was after dinner before we started out, and I wasn't expectin' much. Like we heard yesterday, my guide wouldn't get off a ranger trail. Along in mid-afternoon I had a call of nature, told Jack, and we both got off our horses. I tied mine up by the halter rope. Just in case, I took my rifle out of the scabbard and took it with me and leaned it up against a tree, handy. And what do you know, I just got the job done when not far away came a line of deer, a small buck in the lead. I had time to kneel down, take aim, and shoot, and down went that buck."

O'Leary said again, "Yep. We done it that time."

The hunter went on, "It looked like the deer and the shooting didn't scare the horses. They were still there. Jack did a kind of a messy job of dressing out the deer. He cut his throat and clear down the belly. We both pulled out the entrails and pulled them away. Neither of us had a meat axe, so we couldn't quarter it. We turned it over, hair side up, and Jack says, 'That'll do for tonight. We'll be gettin' it in the morning'. I says, 'Jack, we oughta brush it up.' 'Whadda ya mean, brush it up?' Well, Claire taught me a good lesson on brushing up yesterday, so I passed it on to

62

Jack. 'We gotta get it up in the air on some limbs so it's off the ground,' I tells him, 'then we gotta get a whole lot of small pine branches to cover it so the birds and the snow won't get to it.' So that's what we did. I'm kind of glad it was a small head, because I couldn't get it mounted anyhow, the way Jack cut its throat. I asked Jack about the liver. Jack says, 'Aw, that's just guts. Let's leave it for the birds.' So we got on our horses and came back to camp."

We got to talking about tomorrow. The hunters, all four of them, said they were kind of tired and thought they'd like a day resting around camp. That was just fine with me. "We got three critters to bring in—two elk and a deer—that's six pack horses. I think us guides will all go out together. In the mornin' we'll go up Carmichael Fork and get that big elk, and on the way back pack up that other elk and bring it in. That's plenty for the mornin'. Then after dinner two of us can get the buck on Grouse Mountain. OK?" .

It worked out pretty much that way. It was a good thing we left two extra pack horses in the corral when we wrangled, because the four we took with us in the morning sure got tired. We went up Carmichael Fork first. Claire did a whale of a job caping out the big bull elk. The quarters were heavy and the big head added to it. It was a ways extra to where my hunter and I left the quarters and head of the other elk. After we got them all to camp, the meat strung up on the meat pole, the heads taken care of and the horses turned out, we were sure ready for dinner.

Claire decided to come along with Jack and me in the afternoon. I welcomed him along, because I knew Jack would be no help. His hunter wanted to go with us—he said he could go right to the deer. When Jack said he was tired, he'd had a hard day the day before, we said nothing at all, and he just stayed in camp.

The hunter found us the meat all right. Of course, it was right close to the ranger trail. We couldn't admire Jack's job of dressing it out, but there wasn't anything we could do about it. We quartered it and loaded it up, and got back to camp fairly early.

Just before Bill called "Come an' get it!" the horse wrangler from the lodge rode in with a note from the boss. "One of our guides out at the South Fork got sick," it said, "and we're short. Can you send us in a good one? Of course you know one man can legally guide two hunters. Tomorrow, send us in what meat you have and that extra guide." After I read it out loud and said, "Jack O'Leary's elected." Nobody clapped, but everybody grinned.

Jack said that was OK with him, he had some things he left at the ranch that he wanted to pick up anyway. He'd help the horse wrangler with that bunch of pack horses loaded with meat and see what he could do to help the boss.

We had an extra bed in camp for the horse wrangler, and he rolled it out in the cook tent. We guides got up before daylight and packed the twelve quarters of meat and the two heads and capes. We picked another big, strong, and gentle saddle horse for Jack and hoped we'd get the horse back. The wrangler said he'd be back before long with the pack horses, because we'd need them, and I asked him to include the saddle horse Jack was riding. We shook hands all around, and they took off. I was relieved that one problem was over.

Now we were four hunters, three guides, and a cook. The hunters stretched and yawned, and said they'd like the afternoon to neaten up their clothes and rest. We would all get up real early for a long hunt. If they were going to do a little partying, that was none of my business; after all, it was their hunt. Claire and I, checking the horses over, found a few loose shoes. We had extra nails for horseshoes, shoes, and hammer in the camp supplies. Charley Johnson came to help, and we found he was a real good hand. We got the job done faster than we expected, and we were all set.

I took two hunters with me, and we rode up Spread Creek toward Pete Hansen's cow camp right under Green Mountain. There were no fresh cattle tracks. We could see he'd trailed them down into lower country already, toward his ranch in Jackson Hole below us. It got colder and began to snow. One of my hunters got a shot at a bull elk, but he missed. He put up with good grace the other guy ribbing him. I'd found out they were all really expert shots and good friends. It got to snowing harder. We ate lunch under the shelter of some big spruce and rested awhile, with our horses tied under the same shelter.

I got to assessing our situation. The camp was in a sheltered spot, even if the wind came up. The feed on the meadows was prime. Even if we had a bad storm and a lot of snow, the horses could easily paw down for grass, and we had plenty oats packed in. The number of elk tracks seemed to show that probably the migration to the Jackson feed ground was already started. That should help the hunters. Both Charley and Claire wanted to go up toward Grouse Mountain with their hunters. I had a feeling we were all going to be lucky.

We were just getting up from lunch, and picking up our rifles to put them in our scabbards on our saddles, when a squealing in the pine timber uphill from us got our attention. Into view came a young calf elk dragging a hind leg. Not far behind it a black bear was coming, looking to jump on its back and kill it. My hunter, cool as can be, pulled his rifle out of the scabbard, and laid it across his horse's rump and aimed. The horse didn't move then, but just as he fired the horse did move, and the bullet went wild. The bear turned and rolled away out of there, so fast you could hardly see him disappear. He shoved his rifle back in the scabbard, cussed himself and said, "Boy, oh boy, I'm gettin' worse."

We were just mounting up when a cow elk, kind of scrawny, come out of the timber and right to the calf, and licked him—must have been her calf. I asked one of the hunters if he wanted that cow. He kind of snorted and said he didn't rob the craddle. The cow herded the youngster back into the timber, and that's the last we saw of them.

We rode on up to Pete Hansen's cow camp—a solid log cabin right in the middle of a big park. It was fenced with a buck fence, beside an island of heavy spruce. Nobody was there, and the tracks of cows were getting snowed up fast. The cowboy had taken the last of his stock down. Snow came down a little harder then. We thought we better turn and go down the Spread Creek trail toward camp—might run into something down that way, you never know. The only things we saw out of the ordinary were three coyotes racing like mad up a hillside across the creek from us. We didn't have any idea what set them off.

About a mile short of camp we saw some fresh elk tracks in the snow, heading south toward the feed ground. It sure looked like the migration had started. It was nearly dark, and the snow was heavier, when here came a line of elk, with a big dark cow in the lead. The hunter who didn't have an elk yet got off his horse, got his rifle, knelt by a log, aimed and fired, and down went that lead cow. The others were gone in a flash. They didn't even see us.

The hunters were a great help. With darkness so close, they knew we were in a hurry. I dressed out the elk and they pulled the entrails off to one side and took care of the liver, wrapping it in the canvas tied to my saddle. By the time I got it quartered with my meat axe, they had the pile of limbs ready to lift the quarters off the ground, hair side up, and a lot of small pine branches ready to make snow protection on top. We were back on our horses and on the trail before it was really dark.

Our cook, Bill, had the horses in the corral already and was starting to grain them when we rode in. I took the job away from him and was barely started, when Claire and his hunter showed up. We lighted a couple lanterns to finish up. We weren't really worried about Cowboy Charley and his hunter, because we knew Charley had a good sense of direction and wouldn't leave his horse, who knew his way even better. And sure enough, here they came.

It kept snowing hard, but the tents were warm and cozy, and everyone had a warm sleeping bag. Pretty soon all you could hear around camp was a bunch of snores. I always tried to be careful, when picking a camp site, to stay away from any dead trees that might blow down. But I got fooled this time. A tree that none of us suspected at all came down in the middle of the night. It fell straight across a hunter's tent, breaking the ridgepole, and landed with its tip on the ridgepole of the cook tent. Scared us all. I knew a lot of cleaning up was ahead of us, and some of it had to be done right away, before daylight.

The tree was a small thin lodgepole, only about four inches across, so we sawed it in about three pieces with the wood saw and lifted it carefully off the two tents. We couldn't do much about the broken ridgepole till daylight and just propped both broken ends up with poles until then, after we shook the loose snow off. The real good fly protected the tent itself. There was a rent in the fly we'd have to sew up tomorrow. Thank God for that new nylon thread! The cook tent wasn't hurt much. We had to do quite a lot of swearing, knocking snow off, tightening ropes, and straightening the stove pipe. We had hardly got the fallen top section back in place and tied down with "Mexican rawhide," when Bill had smoke coming out of it, his lantern lit, and water on for coffee! We all came in to warm up before going back to bed. There was some hot language being used, but the pine tree didn't know about it. We were all sleeping before long and a little late getting up in the morning.

The lateness didn't hurt the hunter's feelings. They said back home they never got up that early—never! So we didn't get saddled up and off until after a good dinner.

It was clear and cold, not a cloud in the sky, and lots of untracked snow around. One of the hunters beat the rest of us eating, pulled on his warm coat and, taking his gun along, sat on the firewood pile just outside. He was puffing on his pipe and taking in the beautiful scenery, when across the park come an animal he never saw before. His gun went off. You can bet all six of us lost no time getting outside. That guy was chasing across the snow, and we chased after him. He had shot a lynx! Pretty scarce any time, and you never could expect to see one.

This was a two-week trip and getting toward the end. Two of the hunters had all the game they wanted. They stayed around camp, had Bill heat some water for them on his little stove, washed their socks, washed themselves, and took a little nip out of their bottles now and then.

The horse wrangler came in again with our bunch of horses, including the big gentle one Jack O'Leary had ridden. I asked him about Jack. He didn't know much but said Jack asked the old lady for a day's rest before he went out to the South Fork—he was tired. She let him get away with it as guides were hard to get. The wrangler said he never saw anyone with a bigger appetite or with bigger stories to tell. He said, "I was polite and acted as if I believed all that gush." Then O'Leary went to South Fork with a guide who had come in with a hunter, and that's the last the wrangler saw of him.

Later my hunter and I were out, when we heard a couple shots down below us. "That's the way Cowboy Charley went," I said. "I hope they connected this time." They had. We were back at the corral early and were there when the two rode in, with big grins on their faces. Charley said, "He got a big cow." The hunter said, "A cow's what I wanted, my wife is gettin kinda fussy about all the room my mounted heads are takin' up, and now we got enough good meat to last us all winter." He grinned at Charley, "And Charley didn't have to get out of sight of his horse, either."

A few days later the wrangler came in with our pack horses and a couple hunters. We were kind of jammed for sleeping space that night, but the next morning we packed all the meat, the lynx skin, and the hunters' gear on the pack horses, said goodbye to the hunters, and called that hunt over.

There was a note in with the grub the wrangler brought. The boss said, "These are two resident hunters. They got money enough, and they'll stay as long as they like. One of you bring them in, with their meat, when they're through. Then finish up your own hunt and tear down the camp. I'll send pack horses back for you." It turned out that Claire and I got lucky right away. Bill shot an elk at early daylight right from the cook tent. Cowboy Charley didn't want an elk. "I don't care for elk meat, and there's plenty of deer near my cabin." The resident hunters got their game right along with us. We used the horses we had left to pack in the hunters' meat and gear, and Bill's stuff. Charley went out with them and came back with the wrangler and the horses we needed to pack out the camp and the rest of the meat.

The wrangler went hunting, and he was lucky, too. Claire and I had everything down but the cook tent, and under cover, because it kept on snowing. The wrangler brought his meat in about the time Claire and Charley and I had the horses all packed and ready to go. My time as camp boss was over.

Flaxie

More than forty years ago I was guiding in a camp where there was a sorrel gelding with a flaxen mane and tail. As I remember, he was called Flaxie, and as I found out later, he seemed dang near human.

The camp was in the Wiggins Fork country, not far under Mt. Kent and close to Caldwell Creek. Eldred Meeks and Bill Jordan from below Dubois ran the camp. The weather was dry and sunny, no snow as yet and plenty of game around. Good feed and a good wrangler meant we had very little trouble with our horses. A fine cook and great weather and lots of game makes a good camp.

Flaxie's owner was a man we called Murph. He showed up while I was guiding for Eldred and Bill, arranged for his hunt, and sat down with us for supper. All the guides and hunters had been admiring Flaxie, so Flaxie was all we wanted to talk about.

"Give you fifteen hundred dollars for that horse, cash down and no questions asked," said one of the oil-rich Oklahoma hunters, first off.

Murph grinned. "Nope," he said, "Just plain nope. First, Flaxie's not my horse. He belongs to my wife. Second, he's part of my family. My wife didn't want me to take him on this trip. I wanted her to come, too, along with Flaxie, but she had something else important to her to do. She finally said I could take Flaxie, if I took real good care of him."

"Where'd you get the horse?" I asked. "He looks like an Arabian—that short back, small feet, dished nose, big eyes, delicate ears, and sensitive mouth. His shiny sorrel coat with flaxen trimmings is a beauty."

Murph looked pleased. "You named him. I was with the U.S. Foreign Service for some years, and most of that time I was assigned in the Near East. One time my wife and I drove through this small Arab village in a desert oasis and saw this colt. Maybe three years old. My wife wanted him

68

right away. We found out who owned him. The family didn't want to sell—he'd been brought up like one of the kids, like you read about. We went on, but we came back with a horse trailer and dickered some more. We had to pay a big price, but we finally got him. He's a gelding, and we didn't find out why they gelded him. Arabians usually don't, you know. They keep them as stallions. Anyway, we love him just like he is."

We got to know Murph pretty well in the next few days. We found out that he and his wife were renting a small ranch in northeastern Wyoming and heard about one they might buy up this way. He liked the idea of combining a look at it with an elk hunt. He had a good pickup and horse trailer, so here he and Flaxie were. Murph got along well with the rest of the hunters, and drank with them some in the evenings.

In a couple of days he and his guide connected with a small elk. He was very happy about it, and the day I'm remembering he and his guide went out with a couple of pack horses to bring it in. I just happened to see him putting a flat whiskey bottle into a saddlebag when I was getting horses ready for my hunter and me.

I was guiding an experienced hunter from Oklahoma. This day, up on the slopes of Mt. Kent, he got both a good elk and a small deer. We dressed out both critters and brushed them up, ready to pack into camp next day. Now he was ready to go back to camp to rest awhile.

We rode down the mountain about the way we'd come from camp that early morning. The other hunters had ridden in the same direction before they'd split off and gone their own ways. We heard a horse walking along parallel to us and stopped to see who it was. It was kind of rough right there, loose rock and grassy sage with scattered lodgepole pine growing in clumps, not really steep, but sure no race course.

We recognized Flaxie right away. He would take a careful step as if to test the footing, then try another. He was walking as if on eggshells, trying not to break them. He was smelling out the trail they'd come up that morning. His rider, Murph, wasn't helping him any. He was grinning happily, his eyes shut, but he had both feet in the stirrups and had a tight hold on the saddle horn.

"Well, I'll be damned," my hunter said. "Drunk as a lord, and on a horse I'd give two thousand for!" As a nurse, Flaxie must have done it before, but I'd never seen a horse capable of what he was doing. I got off my horse and went over to Flaxie and his drunken load. Flaxie gave me a thankful nudge and a low nicker—glad to have some help much needed. I untied the reins from the horn, tested the cinch, and got back on my horse. With my hunter riding close back of Flaxie, and with me leading

him, we rode down to camp a mile or two away. Flaxie led very well. He was sure careful with his load as we crossed the creek to camp.

Murph sort of woke up when we stopped his horse and started to help him off. He said he was OK. He explained that he wanted to come back to camp before his guide got finished putting his meat on the pack horses, and he knew Flaxie could find the way. "You'll take care of Flaxie, give him a good rubdown?" he asked. He staggered toward his tent, so I unsaddled his horse, let him drink his fill at the creek, and gave him a big rubdown. I gave him an extra good can of oats, then turned him loose with the bunch of horses the wrangler was ready to bell and throw up on the hill for the night.

This was the only camp I've ever been in that had a poker game going on for half the night. It ruined the next day's hunting. Meeks and Jordan weren't gamblers. Neither was I nor any of the other guides. (If you are lazy, stay out of hunting camps; it is hard work and you need all the shut-eye you can get.) These were all out-of-state hunters. Murph was happily sleeping off his drunk and wasn't a poker player anyhow.

The next day Murph paid his bill, loaded his quarters of elk and his gear into the pickup, put Flaxie into the trailer, and took off for Dubois, where he'd have the locker plant process the meat into packages for his freezer. He had now completely sobered up.

I happened to be in town when he was ready to drive home. He was just tying down the trap covering the meat and stuff in his pickup, in front of the locker plant. He grinned and we shook hands. He waved toward the horse trailer, where Flaxie's bright eyes were taking us in. "I'm sure taking good care of Flaxie," he said. I just couldn't help answering, "And Flaxie sure takes good care of you!"

I've never heard of Murph again, but I've always remembered Flaxie.

70

Clown

O nce I made a horse trade with a neighbor. She lived a mile or so down the road from my ranch, had a bar and a motel, and took out horseback riders. That fall I dickered with her for about fifteen young horses. None was broke, the oldest was about three, and several were young colts. I made a down payment on them, and told her I'd pay her the rest in the spring. She said, "That's OK, Joe, I'll trust you for it. I'll give you a bill of sale right now, in case you want to sell off some, if you'll keep an eye on my place this winter!" That's the last I saw of her till spring. She took off right away for California.

We had an easy winter. I had enough hay, and the feed in the open was so good we didn't have to hay the horses every day. So the new colts, as well as my bunch of eight or ten, got along just fine. I was building new dude cabins, using the house logs I had cut that summer and fall, so between gentling colts and carpentering, I was plenty busy that winter. My wife, Mary, who loves horses, was a great help in gentling those colts.

In those days, everybody would be trading off what he had too much of for what he didn't have enough of. I had about 150 feet of good inch-and-a-half manila rope I had gotten in a trade. I used it to picket-break the older colts. I like that system. You don't have to do any tricks to halter-break them, they do it all themselves. I dragged three big logs about twenty feet long into the meadow, and spaced them well apart. Then I'd take one three-year-old at a time into the corral, get a halter on him, tie about thirty-five feet of rope by a bowline around his neck, feed it through the ring on the halter, and drag him out to one of the logs. I'd tie the other end to one of the logs with good strong half-hitches and then ride off and leave him. These horses hadn't been touched. They would fight the rope, and you'd have to drag them out to the log. When you left, almost every one would smell the log, then take a run away from it, coming

71

up short at the end of the rope. That's why I used a thick rope, so they wouldn't get rope-burned. Then they would come back to the log, maybe take a second run in a different direction. I've heard of horses once in a while throwing a kink in the neck at this stage, but very rarely (maybe one in a hundred) and none of these did.

They taught themselves all about ropes in a hurry. Once in awhile I'd take each of them a feed of oats and a pail of water. They'd try all kinds of didoes, and they'd learn something each time. They'd get tired, and rest, and look longingly at the mountains, then think up some other trick they could play on the rope, and try it, and learn some more. You might say these horses were in the first grade and getting a touch of education they didn't think they needed. After two days, or maybe three days for the slowest learners, they were halter-broke and picket-broke and not scared of a rope; and they had taught it all to themselves.

I was building cabins on the hill above them and keeping an eye on them all the time. After the first day, I'd see them getting the rope across the back or around a leg, not get excited but stop and study awhile, then carefully untangle themselves. The rope became not an enemy but a friend they could count on. I could see Mary watching out of her kitchen window, enjoying seeing the colts educate themselves.

Every once in a while she'd take a can of oats to the small pasture the yearlings and two-year-olds were in. Almost right away one after another

would learn to watch for her and come running for a handful. She could soon rub each one's muzzle and ears. That sure did help a lot when their turns came on the rope.

One of the fastest learners was a three-year-old we named Clown. After two days on the picket-log, when I untied the rope to take her to the corral, she put her nose right between my shoulders and kept it there, walking along quietly behind. From the looks of her, and from what I knew of Mabel's horses, her father must have been a Hambletonian stallion. She loved to trot and had a great trot. She also looked as if she had thoroughbred in her. She was big and well-built. She was mottled in two shades of brown, a white spot on her forehead continued as a blaze down her face, and she had a white hind foot.

There were only three mares in the bunch, and the rest had been gelded, so I didn't have any trouble with love affairs or originals. We named this mare Clown because she loved to play tricks on you. One of the first she worked out was to get the pellets I often carried in a coat pocket. If I was fixing fences, I'd get hot and hang my coat on a fence post. Clown would slip up when I wasn't watching, pick up the coat and shake it, turning it around in her mouth till the pellets fell out. She was a smart mare, but she never did learn to hang the coat back on the fence post.

Clown had a half-sister we named Susie. Susie was a little smaller than Clown, and Clown thought the world of her. Out in the pasture, the two would be near each other, and if any other horse came near Susie, Clown would drive him away, using her teeth if she thought it necessary.

She turned out to be a one-man horse. I broke her myself, and she always treated me just fine. One time she bucked off Mary. Didn't hurt her, but scared her plenty. Oh, she climbed back up her and finished her ride, like you have to, not to spoil a horse, but she didn't ride her any more. Several other people tried to ride her, but she bucked with all of them, so I decided she was just for me. I fell in love with Clown and it seemed she did with me. I used her for the next ten or twelve years as a saddle horse. I needed more pack horses than saddle horses, and that's what most of the rest turned out to be.

We had a friend, Phil Nebeker, who brought truckloads of fruit over from Idaho in late summer and fall. We would buy crates of plums and berries and stuff. One day when we were looking over his stock, Clown and Susie came trotting up, full of curiosity. Nebeker tossed out a couple of less-than-perfect plums. Clown picked one up, ate it tentatively, and spat out the pit, then went for the other one and looked around for more. She liked apples, grapes, and peaches, but not oranges. Clown was an

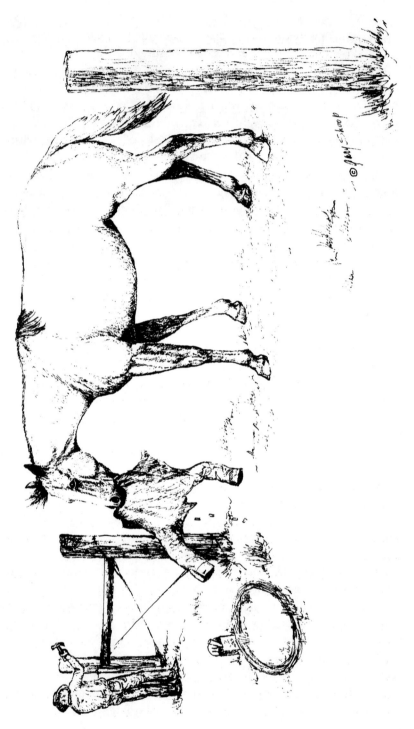

adventurer in food; Susie tried a few of the things Clown liked, but never as eagerly.

One time when Clown was examining my coat, I had no pellets but did have a couple of candy bars. She shook the coat upside down, and out came the bars. She picked one up and ate it with gusto, wrapper and all. By then, I had rescued the other one.

Then once we were trailing a bunch of horses up the road. The horse wrangler was up in front, and Clown and Susie and I brought up the rear. In those days we didn't have trucks or trailers to get horses into the mountains. We drove them along the highway to where the trail took off. I hadn't had enough breakfast and remembered the candy bars I had in my coat pocket. I took out a nutty one and took off the wrapper. Clown heard the paper rattle and stopped dead still. She turned her head around and wouldn't move until I got the idea and broke my bar in half and shared it with her. Before we trotted the fifteen miles or so to the trail head I got hungry again. Once more, Clown heard the paper rattle and stopped until I shared with her again.

In those days I was a tobacco-chewer, and one day, just for the hell of it, I offered her a small slice off my plug. She seemed to like it, so I did it again. I had heard that it was good for horses to have a little tobacco now and then. It was supposed to discourage worms. I don't know how true this is. For a week or so I kept this up. Then one day when I offered her a chew, she bit me! Obviously she was smarter than me. She quit and that's how she told me.

Out in a summer fishing camp on the South Fork of the Buffalo, our whole party was in the cook tent eating dinner. Mary said, "We've just got too many trout—there's more here than we'll eat." She had wrapped them in cornmeal and fried them in butter, and they were plumb good. But she was right, there was more than we could eat. Mary took the leftovers and put them in the dish for the horse-wrangler's dog. The dog was a big handsome German shepherd, not easy to scare. He didn't like it when Clown came around from behind the tent and practically said, "That's for me!" He growled right by her face, but her face was bigger than his and covered the dish. He ran around to bite her heel, and she kicked him—a careful little kick. She didn't break any bones. He came back to sneak a bit off the plate, but by then the trout was all in Clown's stomach, and the dog could only lick the plate.

One time Mary and I were eating lunch in our "river room," the picnic place by Wind River, when Clown and Susie stopped by to see what was up. Just for fun, we offered them each a bit of hamburger sandwich. Susie

75

turned it down. Clown accepted and solemnly chewed hers, rolling her eyes. It went down, and I offered another bite. She took it, too. After that she added hamburger to her list of dainties.

By this time, we got into the art game—painting, sculpture, and writing. We sold the ranch, bought an acreage fifteen miles down the river and built a log home and studio. We sold our horse bunch, but kept Clown and Susie on. The house-building kept us too well-occupied for a while to give us time to build fences and corrals, and Clown and Susie kept pretty close to us. I was using both of them, anyway, for sculpture models and wanted them close by. One day we were inside the studio and heard a knock on the door. We looked out the window, and there was Clown alone at the door. Had she learned to knock? We found a window where we could see what she was doing. Her lips were closed around the door-knob, her head was tilted, and she was actually moving the knob. That didn't quite work. Our experimenter pulled her lips, way back, took the knob in her teeth—and the door came open!

About this time I met Lee Rodgers. A ranch nearby signed him on as a hunter and looked me up for a guide for him. We had a good hunt. He got both an elk and a bear, and he fell in love with Clown and Susie. He came to Wyoming several years in succession, and every time he would look us up and get re-acquainted with the horses. He wanted to buy them and offered us a good price. He was a manufacturer of automobile parts in Ohio and had a country place with lots of bluegrass pasture. He would truck them to Riverton, he said, and ship them east in a box car. They would be happy on his place, he assured us. He didn't mind that they were getting old by now. He just wanted them.

We had to take him seriously. After all, our five acres wasn't much pasture. We had to buy a lot of hay and grain, and prices were going up. So we gave in. It made sense, but we've always been sorry. Mary and I both wept when we saw that truck go down the road. For several years, Lee kept sending us word about them. They must be long gone by now, but our eyes still fill up when we think about them.

Whetstone Mountain

One fall, a couple years after I'd quit guiding, Mary and I decided we needed a good elk apiece to last us the winter. We were both enthusiastic meat eaters, and it took a lot to satisfy our ferocious appetites.

By this time we'd sold our ranches and moved to five acres on Wind River east of Dubois and built a cabin or two on the land.

I'd loaned my good tent and hadn't gotten it back. A friend offered us his, a 10x12 wall tent. "It's pretty near new, it's in good shape, and here it is." It was all rolled up, it did look new, and we took his word for it.

The rest of our equipment was pretty much collected: grub for several days, warm sleeping bags (by now these replaced the old-time bedrolls), and the best winter outfits we could locate—wool pants and shirts, down jackets, caps with warm ear-flaps, and especially good stout packs with wool socks. We didn't have horses, and we weren't jeep hunters. We knew we'd camp at the edge of the wilderness—the end of the road—and we'd have a lot of walking to do. We put in a small barrel of gasoline for the pickup, a small camp stove and stove-pipes to fit, rope, and two or three extra tarps. We had a conglomeration of tools—car tools, shovel, axe, saw, extra battery, and other small items that would come in handy in camp, like plenty of baling wire (Mexican rawhide, we called it) and pliers to use it.

The day before, we took the pickup in to Dubois to get it looked over. Our friend Slim at the filling station, a big tall fellow from Texas, fresh out of the Air Force, said to me, "I've got a new jeep I've been wanting to take hunting. How about it—can I go with you? I need an elk, too, this winter." I said, "OK. Glad to have you." He was a good hand, a real helper, and fun to be with.

The next morning we started early. When we went through Dubois our friend fell in behind us with his jeep. The highway was a little slick, but not bad. We headed over ToGwoTee Pass and for Pacific Creek, where a forest service road turned off toward Whetstone Mountain. It was a single-lane gravel road, but not bad, and we followed it several miles to a good camping spot near the mouth of Murie Creek, a couple of miles from the wilderness boundary. A mile or two before that spot, we passed a small hunting camp. I knew it belonged to a man from Moran who was in the business of packing out meat for hunters who didn't have horses. I knew Frank Foster, and we stopped to howdy with him. I told him where we planned to camp—by those big spruces close to the mouth of Murie Creek—and we hoped to get us three elk, one apiece. If we were lucky, and came to him for help, how much would he charge to pack them out? He said, "Oh, twenty or twenty-five dollars apiece." I said, "That's fine. We'll hope to see you in a day or so."

As we went to get into the pickup and the jeep, we passed Frank's gear tent. In the door of it was sitting a young guy working on a saddle—a tall young man maybe nineteen years old. He was sitting on the edge of the tent floor in the warm sunlight. He squinted up at me and grinned. He said, "Howdy," and we howdied him back. I said, "I see you're a good hand with a saddle." "Yes," he replied. "We got a couple resident hunters out now, from Cheyenne. One is a big fat guy who is putting cinch sores and kidney sores on every horse he rides. He has to ride a big horse. We change horses for him every time he comes in. I'm going to teach him how to ride a horse straight up—I mean, *right*." This was about twenty-five years ago, my memory may be at fault, but I'll never forget this boy. "That's quite a job, son. How you figger on doin' that? I'd like to learn somethin'." Frank Foster was grinning behind us. "Yes, let us in on it, Tom. I need to learn that, too."

Tom said, "I notice this guy mostly sits on the left side of the saddle. He hardly ever rides straight up like any damn fool oughta know. So I'm lengthenin' the left stirrup. That way, it'll be too *damn* long, and to balance he'll have to sit over and use the right stirrup like he oughta. They always come in at noon, they get too hungry. That'll give me a chance to switch saddles on him."

Frank followed us over to our vehicles. "You know," he said, "that kid is either going to turn out to be a bank robber or a president. It'll be interestin' to see which, if we live that long."

It started spitting snow, so we hurried along to the place I had picked. While we were setting up the tent, Slim said, "This is the durnedest tent I ever saw. It's well put together and well-sewed, but I never saw a tent before that was made outa cheesecloth instead of canvas.

78

Well, it quit snowing so before dark we finished our supper, and by dark we blew up our air mattresses, rolled out our sleeping bags, and hit the hay. Sometime later, Tex punched my side, through the sleeping bag, enough to wake me up. "Joe," he said, "it's snowing' or rainin', and I'll bet it's wetter here than it is outside." I agreed with him. "We got an extry big tarp in the pickup," I said. "Les go stretch it over the tent." Mary held the flashlight while Slim and I got the tarp over the ridgepole of the tent and tied down. It did cover most of the top of the tent. It was still snowing, but not blowing, thank God. Mary got a fire started by flashlight and a couple candles. We had to pull all the stuff away from the wet eaves into the middle of the tent. We got dried off a little before we got back into bed.

Slim and I got up early. There was about four to five inches of very wet snow on the ground—fine tracking snow. We started down the creek, as we knew the elk had started migrating, and thought we might get lucky. We did. We'd hardly gone a hundred yards from camp when we saw a little bunch of elk just crossing a park ahead of us. We both shot. Slim dropped a fine six-point bull, but I missed the fat cow I was aiming at, and the rest faded off into the timber.

I helped Slim dress out his elk and asked him if he had a meat axe for quartering it. He did. I said, "I'd like to stay right here, in case some more come through. Why don't you bring your jeep down, with the meat axe, and we'll quarter yours up, take it back to camp and hang it up to cool out." Meanwhile I crouched behind some brush, looking for more action.

Any other elk around must have been scared off by those two shots. Slim and I both shot Winchester ought-sixes, and they're pretty noisy when there's no wind. When Slim brought the jeep back we quartered the elk up and loaded on the quarters and the head, tied down the load, and took it back to camp. We found poles stretched between the spruce trees that had been used before, so we hung the quarters from one of them. We hung the head up high so it was safe, a fine-looking six-point head.

It was near noon by then and had cleared off and gotten colder. Mary had a hot fire going in the tent, which sure felt good to us. We enjoyed dinner and drying out, before we went out hunting in the afternoon. I put my hand axe on my belt—we might not be lucky so close to the road this time. We climbed a small hill, came into an open aspen patch, and sat down on a log to rest. Here came a big bull out of the timber into the aspens. He shook himself, turned around, looked behind him, and bugled. He wasn't the fat cow I wanted, but, hell, I might never get a better chance, so I shot, and down he went. Slim said, "This is sure our lucky day. I can drive the jeep to the bottom of this hill. I betcha we can quarter him out, and on this snow, we can drag the quarters down the hill that far. You can save the twenty dollars from Frank Foster."

Slim helped me dress out and quarter the bull, then took off for camp and the jeep. Just in case, I had about thirty feet of ⅜-inch rope wrapped around my middle. It comes in handy lots of times, and it sure did today. I tied it on to a hind quarter and dragged it to the hill and then down. It's always hard work dragging quarters of elk, but with this snow and part of it down a steep hill, it wasn't too bad. I stopped to rest every once in a while. Before long I could hear Slim's jeep engine.

Slim was a good jeep driver. There was no road, but he angled around and got almost to where I was waiting. The two of us got the rest of the meat and the head. It was a plenty tight fit to get them loaded into the back of the jeep, but we managed it, tying them in place with that ⅜-inch rope.

Slim asked, "Are you always this lucky, Joe?" I told him, "I should say not. I kind of expected to get skunked. We are sure helped by being right where the migration is comin' through." It was beginning to get dark, so we didn't linger. Slim followed his own jeep tracks back to camp. We tested the other meat pole that was already in place for us. It seemed strong. Slim drove the jeep right under it, and we hoisted up the meat and head, using our extra ropes and some of that "Mexican rawhide."

Mary proudly showed us the result of her work that afternoon—a big stack of firewood, enough for all night and part of next day. We sure had a good supper, sitting around on our rolled-up sleeping bags near the hot stove—fresh elk liver, spuds and prunes, and other good stuff on our tin plates, and coffee to go with it.

Slim said, "It's your turn, Mary, tomorrow. You've got to get us a cow. Me, I'd like to stay and help, but I've got my elk, and I'd better get back to keep my job. Jobs are scarce this fall, and I'm lucky to have one. Besides, I've got to bare off that meat pole for Mary's elk. Listen!" Close to us, an elk bugled, and we could hear other sounds of movement not far off.

We both thanked him for his help. We'd miss him tomorrow, him and his jeep, both. But we were two able-bodied people, and with the migration to help us, with our pickup, and with Frank Foster in the background, we'd be all right.

It snowed some more during the night and turned colder. The next day Slim helped us tighten up the camp some more, heaping snow and branches around the sides. We helped him load up his jeep. His elk quarters had

80

cooled down. In fact, it was cold enough that they'd stiffened up and started freezing. Slim worried a little about us getting out to the highway and insisted on helping us put chains on the hind wheels of the pickup. Mary put up a good lunch for Slim to take along. In turn, Slim left most of the food he had with him, because he needed the space in the jeep.

Slim waved goodbye, saying that he'd stop at Frank Foster's and if anyone was there, tell them that we were all right. We were a little surprised to find no other hunters nor hear any shooting. Other hunters must have stayed closer to the highway.

Mary had two lunches packed for us. We could hear elk bugling high on the ridge above us, so we started uphill in that direction. We had to stop and rest every once in awhile. We talked in low tones about yesterday's good luck, and we had high hopes for today. Mary's Remington ought-six was not as heavy as my Winchester, but it was still quite a weight to carry, and we were climbing at about 8500 feet altitude where the oxygen was a little scarce. Elk sounds seemed to peter out. We wondered if we were on the very end of the migration, and maybe our lucky time was over. We kept going, seeing plenty of elk tracks and sign, all headed downhill in the direction of Pacific Creek and on to the feed grounds near Jackson.

We went on uphill a couple of hundred yards, when Mary whispered, "I'm afraid I've got to stop. I think I have a blister coming on my heel. I have a band-aid in my pocket, and I think it would help to stick it on." She found a stump to sit on and brushed off the snow. She asked me to hang onto her rifle, while she took off her pack and socks. Sure enough, the heel was inflamed and there was a raw spot. Right then, about a hundred yards away, a handsome elk cow showed up, sideways to us, unconcerned, putting down her head to graze a little bit. Mary got all excited, grabbed her gun from me, knelt behind a nearby log and took a steady aim. We were too close to the elk for me to say a word. I held my rifle ready in case she needed help. Just as she was about to pull the trigger, a bull walked on, right between the cow and us. It was too late. Mary shot the bull! He was dead when we got over to him. The cow had disappeared into the pine timber. It wasn't till then that Mary discovered one foot was bare.

The weather was clear by now, a fine late fall day, but it was getting a bit late, about an hour and a half before dark. We were going to have to hurry. While Mary got her band-aid, socks and pack in place, I cut open the elk's belly, and he bled real good. He was a five-point bull, but we didn't need the horns, so I cut off the head, right behind the jaws, with the meat axe from my belt. We pulled out the entrails, stomach and so on, pulling them some distance from the meat, so any birds would have something to feast on before they went for the meat. We saved the big liver (one of the most delicious parts of an elk), and after we had the quarters taken care of, hid it under some pine branches close by. I cut the meat in quarters with the hand axe, leaving the skin on. Mary helped me turn the quarters over, hide up, close together on some pine branches, to keep the warm meat from the wet snow. Then we cut a lot of small pine branches and heaped them over the quarters, both to protect them from snow that might fall before we could get them out and to hide them from birds.

Mary got kind of nervous about now. "Joe, are you sure you know right where we are? I sure don't. Do you know where camp is, and Frank Foster's camp?" "I sure do," I told her. "After all my years of guiding, if I don't know where camp is I'm sure a fake. We're about three-quarters of a mile from our camp and about a mile and a half from Frank Foster's. As we go, I'll put a few little blazes on trees to guide us back tomorrow, and you'll see, we'll have other help tomorrow. We'll hear all the birds squawking and fighting over the entrails. We can't lose. We'll have camp robbers and moose birds and ravens and chickadees, and maybe an eagle or two."

It wasn't very long before we reached camp. Just dark. I hit it right on the nose. How could I lose? There was Pacific Creek, there was Murie Creek, there was Whetstone Mountain. It would have been different in fog; but even so, Mary was a little surprised. We had a good supper by lantern light and a real good sleep.

Happy about our hunt, we didn't get up too early, just about daylight. Mary wanted to go with me to Frank Foster's so we took off afoot as soon as breakfast was over. Frank was alone in camp. We told him about Mary's bull. "I'm alone here right now," he said. "That big kid, Tom, who works for me, got a fat cow up on the ridge yesterday. He's gone to pack it in. He's pretty happy about it. But I can go after yours right away. I've got enough horses in the corral for us—three saddle horses and two pack horses. Where is your meat and how far?" I told him, something like a mile and a half. He didn't need to go clear to our camp, we could intersect our trail right from here, and I'd left enough small blazes to guide him. Sure enough, we hit the blazes and our tracks, and it wasn't long before we heard the birds. I helped Frank load the quarters on the two pack horses. "I can see you've done this before," he says, grinning. "Sure have. Made my living at it for a good many years."

We made a procession down to our camp without any trouble. As we

82

came out of the timber onto the trail I saw two pickups stopped by ours, and four men in red outfits looking our camp over. One was checking the four quarters of meat on the pole, one had unfastened the ties on our tent flap and was sizing up the inside. I said, kind of grumpy, "If you want some elk, you better go hunt 'em." They didn't like it much, and got in their pickups and rumbled on up the rough road.

I said to Frank, "That's what this country's comin' to. Three days left of the season. Disappointed hunters don't care where they get their elk."

Frank says, "I agree with you, Joe. I better get back to my camp. Who knows what's happened there."

"Hey!" I said, "I owe you money. How much?" He told me and I paid him. Then he unloaded Mary's meat into the pickup, and said, "Now let me help you with the quarters on the pole." "Hell, no," I says, "Thanks anyway. We can drive the pickup right under the pole and lower the quarters into it. You better hustle up into your camp and look it over. We'll take our tent down and clean everything up. Then in a couple hours or so we'll stop by your place and see how it all is with you."

We ate a quick lunch, lowered the elk quarters into the pickup, packed all the camp stuff in around the meat, took down the tarp and the tent and spread them on last, over the whole load, and roped everything down snug. While we were checking over the campsite, to leave everything clean, two pickups went by up the road with four men in red shirts. They didn't stop to say howdy or ask how the hunting was, or even wave, so I couldn't help wondering what they'd been up to. We climbed into our outfit and hurried down to Frank's.

Before we got there, we could see him at his corral, with the kid Tom, his saddle horse and two pack horses, starting to unload his meat. We drove over nearby, and they came out. Frank says, "The guys in them last two pickups didn't stop; but they didn't have any manners, either. You sure can't tell what high-binders will do, this close to the end of the season and the end of the migration, too. From now on, we'll always have someone on hand in this camp." We said goodbye and started the motor, when Tom raised his hand up and came closer. "What did you get?" he asked. "A couple of bulls," I said. "We wanted cows, but we took what we could get."

His answer was solemn. "If you'd been where you shoulda been," he pronounced, "You woulda got two cows."

Frank said, "I think he's going to be President."

We had to grin all the way to Dubois.

The Art Game

As far back as I can remember I had fun drawing. I got in trouble in grade school drawing pictures of the teacher. Later on I kept a memo pad and pencil in my shirt pocket, and almost every day I made sketches of whatever occurred to me and mostly gave them away to anybody around that wanted them.

On this dude spread in the high mountains by Brooks Lake I got acquainted with an artist and gave him one of these. I titled it, "Shorty Flick Coming Out of Chute No. 2 on Bad Whisky." Shorty was one of the hands there, famous for his thirst, and I showed Shorty sitting in a saddle strapped to a whisky bottle, urging it along in a rodeo arena. The cork of the bottle had come out, so Shorty's horse was losing some of his vim. Shorty was making the best of it with his spurs.

This artist was Louis Agassiz Fuertes. He painted birds and was right then working on an article for the *National Geographic* magazine. He had a rifle he called a Marble Over-and-Under. It shot a .22 shell from the upper barrel and BB shot from the lower one. His program was to walk into the forest of lodgepole pine with his daughter and come back with some beautiful little birds that none of us had ever seen before. He'd get out his water-color set (much like one I'd used years ago in school) and make beautiful paintings, making the birds look as if they were really alive. Then he would skin each bird, just so, being very careful about the eyelids, fill it with cotton, smooth it all down to perfection, and tie a descriptive label on its feet. He called these his "collection of museum skins."

Well, he got quite a laugh out of the Shorty Flick drawing and asked if I could show him any more. I borrowed several back from some of the hands and dudes and spread them out. Most of them were kind of comical joke-type cartoons, some were drawings of people, and some were more serious landscapes and animals. I was especially fond of drawing horses.

84

Louis Fuertes laughed at all the funny ones, then he got real serious. "Joe," he asked, "did you ever consider going to art school? You draw very well."

I was flabbergasted. I didn't know anything about art schools, and didn't even think about any kind of job except something like working on a ranch. Being a good horse-wrangler was about the top of my ambition, there in the middle twenties. I told Louis as much. "How would I get started finding out about art schools?" I asked, "and how could I ever afford to go?" "Let's take the problems one at a time," Louis said. "First thing is to write for some information. Leave that up to me. I'm thinking about the Art Institute of Chicago for you."

I thought it over and decided it might be a good idea to find out more. Just maybe I might amount to something, make a real career for myself. I was about twenty-six years old. I was in the Navy in World War I. I'd worked around at a variety of ranch jobs. After the War, I filed on and proved up on a 640-acre homestead forty-two miles north of Douglas, Wyoming. I still owned it. Prices for land were very low about then, but maybe I could sell it for enough to go to school.

I told Louis that. I told him I had left home at fourteen, as soon as I was out of the eighth grade and didn't have any high school. I was flattered that he thought there was any kind of a chance for me, and I sure would like to know more.

The fellows around the bunkhouse who lent me those drawings kidded me some—I didn't know if they thought I was a nut, or if they were kind of jealous. Anyway, I didn't think this would amount to anything. I found out Fuertes was a famous artist, and I hoped one time I might be one-tenth as good.

Now, my friends, remember that I'm talking about a long time ago. This was in the middle 1920s, when I was twenty-six, and I'm now 86. My first love was horses and I had some good friends among them. I liked to draw them, but I knew I wasn't much good at it. I had a secret yen to be a cartoonist. I made friends with Paul Gregg, political cartoonist for the *Denver Post*, when he was staying at the Welty Inn in Dubois on a vacation trip. He was fishing in Wind River, which was real good fishing at that time. I confided in him about Fuertes's talk about art school, and he was for it.

A week or so later Louis Fuertes came out to the bunkhouse after supper and called me aside. The first part was bad news. Because I didn't have any high school the Art Institute of Chicago turned me down. My spirits sank, but Louis wasn't discouraged. "That's not the end," he says. "See if you can make a collection of those drawings you showed me—tell the people what you want them for, and I'll bet they'll want to help. I'm sure I can get you in on the strength of the drawings."

I appreciated all he'd done, and I thought he was wasting his time on a jackass. But I went along with his suggestion and begged the use of some of those drawings from the hands and some dudes. A couple of weeks later (mid-August of 1925 by now) here came Fuertes grinning. "Well, we made it," he said, "The Art Institute says you're OK. I've signed you up as a student." "How much does it cost?" I asked him, shivering. "Eighty-four dollars a term," he told me, "and your first term is from September to Christmas."

This was going to take some doing. I had a little money saved up, stuck away in the bank. If I had to, I could maybe borrow some. Then there was my homestead; I could see about selling it. Fuertes said, "You think it over awhile, Joe." About then the cook rang the dinner-bell, and we all trooped from the bunkhouse to the kitchen. I could hardly eat anything for trying to straighten out my thoughts. After it got dark and I got into my bedroll, I couldn't get to sleep at all. I'd always been sort of a gambler with my life. Maybe this was just the right poker hand for me.

Next day I talked to the boss about it. He said, "I'm for you, Joe. You've got stuff in you and I think it's a good gamble. There'll be a job for you here at Brooks Lake next summer."

I looked up Fuertes and told him I was all for it, and thanked him for his help. He slapped me on the back and said, "Glad to hear it, Joe. You'll make it all right. I'll be watching to see how good you do."

So, I stored my saddle and bedroll there at the ranch and went down to Lander and bought a suitcase and some dude clothes—overcoat and such. I took the train to Douglas and sold my homestead for what I could get. It wasn't very much, and it took me a few days to do it. But soon I bought a ticket to Chicago and got there just about two days before school started.

Well, I got signed in at the Art Institute, found a place to live near enough to walk, and I was off. It wasn't long before I was sure some of the things they were teaching me wasn't what I wanted to learn, and I got awful homesick for the mountains and pretty near took off. But I gritted my teeth and stayed. By Christmas time I realized all of a sudden that my money was going faster than it should—I just didn't know how to handle it. I was going to have to find a way to make more.

I'd heard about people getting scholarships, but I didn't have any idea how to go about that. I just needed a couple of jobs to keep body and soul together. There was another student from Wyoming in my class, and we got to be pretty good friends. I asked him if he knew how to get any kind of a job without giving up school. "Why, yes," he said, "I've got a job, from 4:30 to midnight, pushing an express wagon around, for 42¢ an hour. Come on down with me tonight and I'll introduce you to the boss. It's hard work, let me warn you."

So that afternoon we took a street car and went down together to the freight docks of the American Express Co. near the Northwestern Station. My friend took me to a big Swede about six feet two inches tall and tougher than Jack Dempsey must have looked. He said to him, "This is a friend of mine who needs a job. Hope you can help him. Name's Joe Back. G'by, Joe." He took off, went to a locker, changed his clothes, grabbed an express truck and disappeared.

It was awful cold, like it can get in Chicago in winter. There was a lot of noise, express wagons rattling past, horses backing wagons into docks, men cursing at them. The boss didn't even look at me. He just said, yelling to be heard above the noise, "Can't use you! Have all the help I need! You'll have to go somewhere else." And he turned away from me.

I was desperate. I didn't go away. I punched the big guy in the briskit through his heavy coat, and yelled right back at him, "Listen, mister, if you don't hire me, the American Express Company's liable to go broke! I'm the best damn workman you'll ever see! I'm about as tough a hand as ever come over the pike!" I was down to two meals a day, and hungry. I dreamed that up all of a sudden, and it really helped me out. For the first time, he looked down at me, out of the palest blue eyes I ever saw. "Well, I've heard everything now. I'll yoost call your bluff, by the yumpin yimeny Yesus!" He sent a big wad of snoose right past my ear. "I'll yoost take you on! And, by the yumpin yimeny Yesus, I'll yoost work your ass off!" He went over to a locker, took out a key, opened the door, took out blue coveralls, his size, and said, "You're hired! I'll stake you to these for yoost tonight. Hang that coat in here and have your own coveralls tomorrow or you'll freeze your tail off. The pay is 42¢ an hour, and we pay once a week. Now, get to work!"

I did as I was told. I was thankful I was wearing a warm cap with earflaps and good overshoes and mittens. I hung my coat in his locker, put on his coveralls, rolled the legs up above my ankles, grabbed an express wagon, pushed it over to the nearest dock, and started to unload. I glanced over at the boss, and saw he had his eagle eye on me. There were some trucks hauling boxes, but most were horse-drawn drays backed up to the docks. The man I was close to said to his partner, "Ha! a green hand!"

Then he told me how to sort out the boxes and where to take them. There were all sorts, shapes, and sizes of packages, and of course they each had an address and had to be taken to a special place. I was slow about that part, so to make up, I rushed as fast as I could through the loading and unloading. Every once in awhile I'd catch the boss's eye on me again, and I'd work a little harder. I was soft, of course, having been at school for three months.

By the time midnight came I was shaking, and hardly able to walk. I did manage to take off the boss's coveralls, hang them up, and get into my coat. My friend came by and said, "You don't need to work *that* hard, Joe. The boss has a heart of gold, but he tries to hide it. See you tomorrow." He went off as the boss came along. The boss said, "Get you some better mittens and your coveralls, and be here by 4:30. Goodnight."

I just barely crawled onto a streetcar and got off at the right place, got into my room and flopped on the bed, without taking off my overcoat.

The next night things went a little better. About eleven o'clock the boss came around and surprised me with a big grin. Then the third night he says, "OK, Joe, take it a little easier. We don't want to take care of any dead artists fallin' around here. I don't think the American Express Co. is goin' broke, if we can hire enough hands like you!"

I'd been wondering if an art education was worth the pain I was going through. I stuck with it mainly because I couldn't stand the thought of being kidded for quitting if I went back now. As it was, I worked there three winters and got to be good friends with the truckers, teamsters, and other hands—and the horses, too.

* * *

That was my first scholarship. I was getting along pretty well in art classes. Even the things I thought I didn't need—like design, composition, and history of art—I was finding I did need. I was plunging into figure drawing, charcoal rendering, and anatomy.

But I was still short of cash. I was holding my landlady off, when my friend from Wyoming looked me up again. "Hey!" he said. "I found another good job. If you're interested, come along with me." He walked me very fast into the Loop, explaining as we went: "This is carrying dishes an hour and a half at noon at a Harmony Cafeteria. There must be a dozen of them in the Loop, and the one I work in is close by. I get two 60¢ meals for this dish job, and, believe me, it helps. I'll introduce you to the floorlady, and maybe you can get a job, too, if you want to."

That was the way it worked out. I must have carried enough dirty dishes to stack our house plumb full. You hung your coat on a rack when you came in and put on the cafeteria's white coat instead. After you got acquainted with the girls behind the counter, when you put your own coat back on it felt heavy, and you'd find the pockets loaded with sandwiches and cake. The girls would say, "You look half-starved." The two 60¢ meals were breakfast and dinner, and with the extras in the pocket I began to put on a little weight.

Things were smoothing out. I wasn't so hungry any more. School was getting more interesting. I wasn't thinking of going back to the mountains right away. Then something happened that shook me up. I was carrying a big heavy trayful of dishes when a man got up from right in front of me and knocked that tray right out of my arms. There was a loud clatter, most of the dishes broke, and the floorlady came rushing over. The grapevine said that she was just then getting a divorce, and she was everybody's enemy. She says, "Back, you get your second meal you got coming, then you leave. For good. You're canned!"

That was a real blow. I felt pretty bad. I'd gotten well-acquainted with all the help. I went to say goodbye to them all. Several of them said, "Hey, there's three or four more of these Harmonys just within a few blocks. Why don't you try for a job at another one?"

It was a good idea, and I did just that. The boss at the first Harmony I tried gave me a job right away. I worked there three years. The only mishap was that that boss left, and the replacement turned out to be the same floorlady I'd started in with! She sailed in like a battleship. When she saw me she stopped short, got her memory to working, then she came out with, "OK, Back, so you made it again! Well, keep your mind on the job, keep your nose clean, and you'll do all right."

That was my second scholarship.

* * *

I felt pretty good about things. I was learning about a lot of stuff I never even knew was there to learn. I even got honorable mentions on some of my work. But I could still use more help with finances—and I'll be damned if more help didn't come along!

One day I was picking up dirty dishes from a table where the customer was just getting up, when I realized he looked familiar, just as he was getting the same feeling. "Why, hi, cowboy!," he said. "Last time I saw you, a horse was trying to buck you off, way up there by Brooks Lake! What are you doing here for God's sake?" I busted up in smiles, called him by name and shook hands. It was just quitting time for me, and he waited for me and we visited out on the sidewalk. The upshot was that he said his business was the American Radiator Company on Michigan Avenue, that they needed a watchman for Sundays and holidays, and would I be interested? "The pay is $5.00 for each day; you have to ring bells on each floor and carry a gun and be on guard. But there is some free time when you could study."

He dug out a card and then another one. "Here's my card, and here's the one for the Pinkerton Watchmen's Service. You call them up, tell them I recommend you, give them my phone number, and let's see what happens."

Well, that turned out to be a great help. When I called Pinkerton, they had me come to their office. They phoned American Radiator and gave me a job. They provided a .38 revolver and holster and plenty of instructions. I had a desk on the first floor, and every hour I had to ring a bell on each of four floors and keep my eye on the coal furnace in the basement.

That job lasted all the rest of my Art Institute time. It was mighty useful for study time, if I organized it right. Those were the Al Capone gang war years, when there might have been a lot of trouble. I was just lucky. There were just two scary times. Once while I was at my desk I heard a noise at a first floor window. I took my gun out of its holster and quietly made my way to the sound. Sure enough, a guy was trying to open a window. I got close enough to scare him with the gun, and he ran off down the alley.

The other time was worse. It was Christmas Day, 1927. I was studying at my desk when I was alerted by steps on the basement stairs. I knew somebody got in the basement somehow, and it was my job to see that he got stopped. I took my gun from the holster, aimed it at the middle of the basement door, and pushed off the safety. I didn't want to shoot anyone, but I sure had to be ready. The door opened, and there was the biggest guy I ever saw, and I was aiming right at his middle. Right away I could see he was wearing a uniform and was carrying a huge ring with hundreds of keys on it. I slipped the safety back on fast and yelled, "Hey! Who are you?" He jumped about two feet, then settled down and said he was the Pinkerton watchman who was checking all the places they protected, and he didn't know there was a man on duty here, on Christmas Day. We visited quite a while, till we both got calmed down. I told him, "I haven't yet shot a man on Christmas Day, and I didn't want to start this year." He gave me a big laugh and said he was glad I didn't start with him.

That was my third scholarship. It paid my room rent.

I was still looking around for help. Someone mentioned the art school janitor force, "Old Bill" was the janitor, and he had a crew of about twenty, all students, who gathered up the debris and polished the place up. They worked from seven to nine every morning, and got 41¢ an hour. I hit "Old Bill" up for a job, and he gave it to me right away.

That was my fourth scholarship. Now I was paying my bills as they came along, but I must say I wasn't getting much sleep or much time to study. I was still tempted to quit and go back to horse wrangling in the mountains, but I knew if I did I'd be kidded unmercifully. Summers, of course, I was back there, wrangling horses and guiding, and I sometimes stayed on through hunting season, returning to school in January.

Well, by the time 1930 came around, I was 31 years old and here we were in the Depression. In January that year everyone was blue, but I got my biggest break of all. I was just starting a class in animal anatomy at the Field Museum, a mile-and-a-half walk south of the Art Institute—a class that had been going, of course, since September. In the gallery I looked over the shoulder of a girl making a drawing. "That's a damn good bear," I said, "the best I ever seen." She looked round at me with a glare that froze me and turned away. When the class got together before lunch, there we were both in the same class. That girl looked surprised and smiled—I guess in the gallery she thought I was a tourist instead of a classmate. Anyway, that mile-and-a-half walk was good for courting, and to make a long story short, Mary and I got married a couple years later.

The depression was terrible hard on the art game. Mary had took a job running a wildlife museum out on the edge of Chicago—in the Cook County Forest Preserve. Her boss was Cap Sauers, who'd been a colonel in the artillery. He said to me, "I can get you a job with the National Park Service, building some parks and lagoons north of town. Have you had experience handling men?" I told him what I'd done, and the job took shape, directing a bunch of CCC (Civilian Conservation Corps) men. I got $170 a month and had to provide my own car. I got a used Buick in pretty good shape for $125.00. It had things wrong with it, but I'd made a friend of a good mechanic who was having a hard time getting enough work. He turned this old car into a very fine machine, for which I was sure thankful. Mary was making $100.00 a month. We were so well off that we were very careful not to brag about it—you just didn't in those days. We could live on my pay and put Mary's in the bank. The only trouble was we weren't doing art work.

The depression was getting worse, but our savings account was growing. It went to my head. I had more than my fill of Chicago, and if I couldn't get into art work, I sure as hell needed mountains. Mary was all for it. We made plans for a painting-camping trip in the Buick, back to Wyoming. I had my mind on a small ranch I knew about. We could build some dude cabins, get some horses, run dudes in the summer, hunting camps in the fall, and have time to paint in the winter.

It was quite a plan, but it did work out. Over the years we bought land, built log cabins, barns, fences, ditches. We even did art work in the winter and began to fill painting commissions. We ran dudes in the summer and guided hunters in the fall. Mary became a pretty fair camp cook and loved the mountain trips as much as I did. We worked on this project for twenty years, less two years out for war work during World War II.

Then I began to slow down, and as I went slower, horses seemed to me to go faster. I had accidents—got rolled on, bucked off—the routine hunting camp troubles. I was fifty-five by that time. It was time to go whole-hog into art. Art work began filling our lives.

We sold the ranch, sold most of our horses and camp gear, bought five acres east of Dubois, and built a studio setup. I found out, to my surprise, that I'm a sculptor and worked into a new career. Still, we stayed in the mountains. I worked for other outfitters, took out hunters on trips, continued to enjoy the wildlife, and stayed hooked into the art game.

When I was past sixty, I was chagrined to discover that I could no longer lift up a front quarter of moose to pack on a horse. It was time to retire from packing. About this same time I found out I could set down on paper some of the things I'd learned. I tried writing. Out of the attempts came *Horses, Hitches and Rocky Trails: The Packer's Bible*, a handbook on packing horses. To my great surprise, people bought it. Twenty-six years later, in its twenty-third printing, it still helps out our income. *Mooching Moose and Mumbling Men*, and *The Sucker's Teeth* followed. Now that I'm 86, I'm trying to catch up loose threads and tie it all together.

PART II

THE YOUNG GUIDE FINDS OUT

By Vic Lemmon

"God's Country," bronze sculpture by Vic Lemmon.

Old Moose, the Horse

B ack in the early 1960's, I was working for the Wind River Ranch above town where Sheridan Creek meets the Wind River. That summer a bus company had a package deal worked out for the Audubon group that was staying below town at Trail Lake Ranch. The bus would take them over Togwotee Pass for a float trip down the Snake River, and on their way back they would stop at the ranch for a meal and a horse ride. This was the last trip of the year; it was getting close to hunting season.

First they would eat, then come down to the corrals for their horse ride. Most of the people were over fifty and from back east. I think they would talk each other into the horse ride; some had not ridden for thirty to forty years, and some had never ridden at all.

In this particular group there was a lady who weighed over 250 pounds. I had these two boys working for me all summer—Wylie Eckles, from Texas, and old Harv—both good hands with a horse. Wylie scratched his whiskers and said to me, "Where the hell should we put her?" After some thought we decided to put her on Old Moose and load her last.

Now, some old horses get their names from the way they look. Old Moose was one of them—a strong, big horse, raw-boned and, when he was relaxed, which he was most of the time, his head hung to the ground and his bottom lip was always wobbling. His head was as long as his legs and his eyes were usually shut. The only other state you saw him in was eating. Old Moose would eat anything including the bark off an old pine tree. He had a big Roman nose and a large knot between his eyes, but he was damn sure a good dude horse—kind and gentle—if you just didn't look at him and get the spooks!

After we got the rest of them on their horses, it was time to get that lady on Moose. We got fifty-five, twenty-five, and five-gallon cans and lined them up, in that order, then led Old Moose up to them. This lady, bless her heart, was a very good-natured person and laughed at our ingenuity. But, the big problem was how all three of us were going to help her on without grabbing hold of the wrong places. She was a good two axe-handles across the backside. After some pushing and pulling, we got her on. As she put her leg over the saddle and into the stirrup, Old Moose let out a big groan and lifted his tail and broke wind. This got Wylie laughing, then everyone followed, including the lady.

We got started and everything was going fine until we came out of the pines and into a little meadow. All summer the range cows had made their beds in the middle of it, and it was a dust bowl. When it came Moose's turn to go through the meadow, as usual, he stopped at the edge and ate some old dried grass even the cows wouldn't eat. This stopped all the horses behind him and the ones in front got some distance away.

When Moose couldn't find any more to eat, he lifted his head and started to trot to catch up. This scared the lady and she started to scream. I was in front of the horses, so I turned around and started back to see what the screaming was all about—just in time to see her fall off Old Moose right in the middle of the dust bowl. Now, that damn sure was a sight to see! She hit the ground quite hard. The dust come up in big puffs, like an atomic bomb had just gone off. The dust rolled all around her and up into the sky. By the time the dust cleared, Old Moose had come back and had his nose in her face.

I was really worried, but all it did was knock the wind out of her. She caught her breath and started to laugh about all the dust she had kicked up.

Then came the problem of getting her back on Moose. We found a stump up the trail a little ways that was high enough, dragged a log up to it and led Moose up to the side of it. Wylie, Harv, and I, once again, had to ponder on just where and how to put our hands to keep from getting hold of the wrong places. I decided if I put my shoulder under her instead of my hand it would be safer to help push her back on. As she got on, Old Moose, the clown, went through his show again with the big groan and lifting his tail and everyone got quite a belly laugh.

This was almost the first of September, and hell, here in Wyoming this time of year it can be seventy degrees, and within two hours it can be snowing, and that's just what it did. When we got back to the corral and helped that lady off Old Moose, she put her arms around his neck and hugged him good-bye, then said to us, "With snow coming, spring must be right around the corner." I thought to myself, she damn sure hasn't spent a winter in Wyoming!

96

Bear Scare

I was running a hunting camp for an outfit that was up Lava Creek, between Gravel Mountain and Gravel Ridge. A big grizzly had been hanging around this camp for a few years. In past years, he had torn up the camp a few times, but was wild enough to stay away when people were in camp. I think he would lie back in the timber and wait until the camp was vacant for a couple days, then come in. Back then, you could have a stash in the wilderness. A stash is a little building that is made of pine poles and has to be out of sight back in the timber. Each year after the hunting was over, we would fill it full of pots, pans, stove, stove pipes, etc., but we never left food in it. But, bears have terrific smellers, and Old Grizz must have been able to smell the grease on the stove because every year he would leave new claw marks a half-inch to an inch deep and six to twelve inches long on the stash.

We had the camp set up before the tenth of September. It was now October, and this was the fourth hunt. We came into camp with our new hunters; this was another seven day hunt. When we rode into camp, I could see that Old Grizz had been there. After we unpacked the ponies and took care of them, we looked around to see what Old Grizz had done. We never left food in camp between hunts and carried out all our garbage on horseback so as not to encourage him. We also tied up the tent flaps so when he went in, he could go out the other opening, and, hopefully not make one of his own.

The only thing in camp to eat was horse cake. Horse cake is a pellet about the size of your thumb and very high in protein. The sacks weighed about fifty pounds. Old Grizz had eaten half of a sack while in the grain tent, then left carrying two more. One had a hole in it, so we tracked him into the pines where he had sat down and had breakfast, lunch, and dinner; but, poor Old Grizz didn't know just how potent that snack was going to be. He must have eaten another half sack and then got one hell of a bellyache because there was bear dung all over the place. You could follow him on a run because he left a stream of bear dung and smell all the way up the mountain, across the meadow, and I don't know how much further because we got such a belly laugh out of it that we wore ourselves out. That night, in the cook tent, the talk was, of course, all about bears. It seems that everyone has a grizzly story to tell, and some had a gunny sack full of them.

One of the hunters told a story of two hunters in Montana; they were hunting elk in the Bob Marshall Wilderness when they came upon a big grizzly. This is back when you could hunt grizzly in Montana. They shot and wounded him, and he rolled down the canyon and into the brush with the hunters right on his trail.

After the grizzly went a mile or so, he made a little circle and sat down by the side of the trail to wait for them. He did not have long to wait before the hunters got there, all excited about getting that grizzly. As they passed by, the grizzly jumped out and mauled and killed one of them. The other hunter shot him three more times and ran, hell-bent-for-election back to camp, caught his horse and saddled it with old Mr. Grizzly right on his tail. He shot it again and down country he went, as fast as his horse could run, to get help.

When they came back, the grizzly was dead, but before he died, he tore that camp to hell. They found five bullet holes in him.

My two hunters were from New York; one was a doctor, we called him Doc, and the other's name was Fred. I could see that Doc was swallowing everything, hook, line, and sinker, so I laid it on pretty thick when I told him about the time I lived in Montana.

A friend of mine was guiding in the Bob Marshall area and they were on, what they called, the China Wall. That's the part of the Continental Divide that runs through here. It goes up gradually from the west side, but drops off into cliffs on the east side. They were on their bellies lying right on top of the China Wall and watching some elk feed in a meadow down on the east side with their field glasses. All of a sudden, the guide got the feeling that something was behind him; he turned around and right at his feet was a grizzly bear cub. He did not want to shoot the cub, so he just hollered at it. But, the damned cub, instead of running away, ran over to the left side of them. Just then, out of the timber came mama grizzly growling and on the fight.

He got up on his knees, but there was no place to run. Behind them was a cliff and in front was the mama grizzly coming at them on the run.

He started to shoot her with his magnum pistol. He hit her all six times, but she just kept coming until she got right to them and fell dead on top of the hunter.

After the guide quit shaking, he rolled the grizzly off the hunter. That hunter was so scared that he couldn't talk or walk, so the guide put him over his shoulder and started carrying him to the horses. Just then, the cub ran up and bit him on the leg and took off a piece of flesh. He dropped the hunter and shot the cub. The poor hunter didn't get his voice back until the next day and, by then, had developed a stutter in his speech and still had it the last time the guide saw him.

Some of the hunters were having a few beers, including Doc, and it wasn't long before nature called. Just as Doc went out of the tent someone said, "Watch out for the bears!" Well, Doc sure changed his mind and did an about-face, came back in, and sat down for awhile until Mother Nature could wait no longer. Then, he asked his partner, Fred, if he would consider going to the outhouse with him. Fred said he had to go too, so this time I gave them my flashlight—a damned good flashlight, too! It had a loose connection and only worked half the time. When they got outside the tent, the light went out, but they couldn't wait any longer. The outhouse was about a block from the cook tent.

We had a horse called Lonesome. Hell, I gave him that name because he was the most lonesome horse I had ever seen. I never belled or hobbled him because he always bedded down in the middle of camp. Most horses sleep standing up, but not old Lonesome, he laid down. If he had a bell on, he would manage to ring it all night just outside my tent. When old Lonesome got spooked, he would run up to you and sometimes over you. When I traded for him, the woman who owned him said she had raised him on a bottle because his mama died when he was born. I think old Lonesome thought he was part human.

Anyway, the doctor and Fred were trying to find their way to the outhouse in the dark when they stumbled over old Lonesome lying right in the pathway. Doc fell right on top of him. It scared old Lonesome as bad as it scared them. Doc and Fred thought a bear had them for sure. Doc let out the most blood-curdling scream I've ever heard.

Old Lonesome jumped up and went to Fred for protection, but Fred turned around and started running and wrapped himself around a pine tree, then fell backwards on the ground. Old Lonesome ran up to him and stuck his nose in his face. If Lonesome had been a racehorse, he still couldn't have caught Fred even though Fred was running on his hands and knees.

Fred came flying into the tent on all fours and went right under the table screaming, "Oh, God, help me! Help me!" I think Fred became religious on the spot. Old Lonesome was right behind him so I jumped up and hollered and whacked him on the nose to keep him from coming in the tent. Lonesome turned around and went back looking for the doctor. He needed some companionship!

Poor Doc, by this time he was trying to figure out which way to go to get away from the bear. When he heard, and could see, this big, black figure coming to him, Doc let out a scream you could have heard clear back in Dubois. He turned around and ran smack-dab into the outhouse. He got back on his feet just as Lonesome put his nose to Doc's hind end. Doc didn't know how he got on top of the outhouse, but there he was and screaming, "Oh, Lord, help me! Help me, Lord!"

It's a good thing Doc had his black bag along because he and Fred both needed a nerve pill. This whole ordeal scared old Lonesome so bad, he must have remembered he was a horse, because he ran out of camp and never came back the rest of the night. In fact, it took us four days to find him!

I know one thing for sure, after that little predicament, Doc and Fred felt like they had been "rode hard and put away wet." I suppose there is something to learn from every experience. Doc and Fred taught Lonesome he was a horse and old Lonesome put the fear of God back into both of them. I know one thing, for sure, they were two humble hunters the rest of the hunt.

Howling Coyotes and Dead Elk

A couple of years have gone by since I guided Doc and Fred. I was still running the same old camp and old Grizz was still visiting us now and then, but, for some reason, he seemed to have lost his appetite for horse cake. This bear had a paw that was about twelve inches long and eight inches wide. In fresh snow it would give you the willies.

It was the end of October and had started to get cold. It had snowed eight inches and had been snowing all night, but by morning it had cleared off. It was a perfect day for hunting; you could really see the fresh signs. There were two hunters: Jim, an accountant, was from California, and Mike, a diesel mechanic, was from Reno, Nevada. Mike was strong as an ox. He had gotten his elk the first day (a nice five-point) so he was riding horses, looking the country over and helping around camp.

Ole Ahlberg was one of the guides from Dubois. He was part Norwegian and part Swede, spoke with an accent, and was a hell of a guide. His father had settled in this country back in the tie-hack days. The tie-hacks were very proud people and could put out a good day's work. Ole's one hunter had his elk so he had one hunter to go.

When the migration is on, that meant good hunting, and it was on! This camp sat right in the middle of a heavy migration route from Yellowstone Park to Jackson Feed Grounds and about ten miles from the Park line.

Our other guide's name was Slim. He was part Indian and came from around Casper—a good guide and a hell of a hand with a horse. Both his hunters had gotten their elk, and he had taken them out.

My hunter, Jim, and I left camp early that morning. Jim had had two different chances to get an elk in the last three days but had gotten too excited. He missed one, and the other time he jerked his rifle out of the scabbard so hard it went flying backwards down the mountain in the snow.

After an hour of traveling in snow almost up to the horse's knees, we came out into an opening that drained into Pacific Creek. The elk signs were everywhere; it looked like a herd of sheep had crossed through. Those elk were on the move and heading south. I knew this area quite well and knew the elk would be in black timber for three or four miles. Jim got all excited about tracking them, but I didn't pay him much attention as I had seen him excited before. Hell, I damn sure didn't want to ride three or four miles in black timber and over downfall with all that fresh snow! You sit just high enough on a horse to knock all the snow off the trees down your neck, in your face, and in your lap.

With two horses and Jim going through that timber, old Mister Elk could hear us coming for a mile. Besides, Jim was a little out of shape and old Dad Time had put some age on him, so that left out walking. Here in Wyoming the air is so clean it's like the breath of an angel and with fresh snow, you can see for miles.

We could see elk coming off Big Game Ridge which was clear on the other side of Pacific Creek. We were about seven miles from Two Ocean Pass; that's where Pacific Creek and Atlantic Creek start. Two Ocean Pass is on the top of the "Backbone." In this country the Continental Divide is called the "backbone" because we think it's the backbone of the world.

With our spotting scope we could count about thirty head of elk with seven bulls, and four of them were damn sure trophies. But they were still a good eight miles off (only four by the way the crows fly, but we were riding ponies not crows). The elk were on the move and would be out of the country by the time we got over there, and, in this snow, it could be dark by then.

Jim, being from California, wanted to try to get up to them, so just to humor him, I rode off in that direction. We hadn't gone a mile when we ran into a herd of elk crossing right in front of us. Jim was riding an old horse named Looker. He got that name because he looked at everything. He would put his ears forward, then look and snort. That gave you the feeling that he might jump away from whatever he was looking at, but he very seldom did. He'd just look and snort.

I told Jim to hurry and get off. Well, he was sure trying, but he got so excited that he stuck his foot up along side of old Looker's neck and got it tangled up in the lead rope and couldn't get that leg over the saddle. By now, his other foot slipped out of the stirrup and went forward down in the snow about even with Looker's head. His right foot was still tangled up in the lead rope and hung up over the saddle horn. Poor Jim's head was back by the horse's flank but he was still trying to reach up and get

102

his rifle out of the scabbard. What a tangled-up mess! Old Looker managed, somehow, even though his lead rope was tight, to put his head down in a position so as to look under his belly and give old Jim a wild-eyed look and snort.

By now the elk had disappeared like smoke in the woods, but Jim was saying to me, "Don't let that big one get away! Don't let that big one get away!" After a few tries I finally convinced him they were gone and to settle down so I could help him get out of that tangled-up mess. I got him untangled and sat him on a log, but he still wanted his rifle. So, I walked back to old Looker, who was still looking at Jim and snorting, pulled out his rifle, and unloaded it. I thought that, in his excitement, he might shoot a horse or someone—mainly me. I got my horse and went over to Jim to give him his rifle.

When a herd of elk are moving, sometimes part of them will stop and feed then catch up later. It looked like that's what had happened, because here came three more bulls right in the tracks of the others. Old Jim jumped up and started working the bolt on the rifle, as if he had shells in it! He'd pull the trigger and say, "I got him!" Then, with no shells, he'd do it again and say, "I got him!" I jumped back to my horse and got my rifle and gave it to him, but I had to jerk his rifle away from him. I said, "Jim, shoot him again because he doesn't know you hit him all those times." He almost floored me! He shot, said, "I got him!" and damn sure if he didn't. He was the smallest bull of the three, but a fat four-point.

Jim told me that he wanted the hide. He was still quite excited, but insisted on helping me dress him out. With Jim helping me, I almost cut my finger off, not once, but three times, so I said, "Jim, I can skin this elk myself; it comes with the hunt. But, if you want to help it will cost $3,000 plus all doctor and hospital bills." Jim laughed like hell over that. He was one happy hunter. He had been hunting elk for twelve years and this was the first one he had ever bagged. I think I can guess why.

By the time I got the elk quartered up it was getting late so we moved out. That night in camp, Ole's hunter decided to stay in camp and rest the next day, so Ole said he would help me get Jim's elk. The next morning we saddled up and went off for the elk.

I decided to take a short cut through a little canyon. After traveling a couple of miles, off to our right, up on a side hill were a bunch of coyotes howling. In the middle of them lay a big, dead six-point elk. He was right on the skyline and just above him, silhouetted, was a big coyote howling. He had his head turned high towards the sky and you could see his breath when he howled. The sight of it chilled me through.

I figured that the elk had been wounded a week or so before and had come this far before dying. In later years I made a bronze of that sight. I called it "Hard Winter." I will remember that sight as long as I live.

We went on to pick up Jim's elk. After we got him in the panniers and hung on the pack horse, we put the antlers on top. I asked Ole to hold them there while I got a rope out of my saddle bag to tie them down. Well, Ole is a little on the short side and when the pack horse moved, Ole was too short to hold the antlers on, and down they came right on top of him. One horn banged him on the head and the other stuck him in the side and drew a little blood. Ole kicked them and cussed like hell; I had to laugh. Then, we tried it again, that time we succeeded with no trouble.

On the way back, when we reached the spot where the coyote and the dead elk were, I decided to go up and get those horns. So, Ole and I rode up there. I got off my horse and tied him up, gave Ole the pack horses and got my meat ax out. I went over by the elk and that's when I discovered the grizzly tracks. Wow! They looked big in fresh snow. I thought he would have been hibernating by now, it was cold enough. Mother Nature makes the bears awfully hungry just before they den up so they will eat enough to last all winter, and, in Wyoming, that is a long time. I guess Old Grizzly needed some more food so he was feeding on this elk.

It's not the smartest thing to do—messing with bear food. I knew better, but wanted those horns, so I took them off the carcass and started walking back to the horses. Just then Ole saw the bear tracks. He really got excited and started to stutter and said, "L-l-look at those b-b-big bear tracks!" His eyes got bigger than saucers and he started to point in my direction. Just then I heard something behind me. The hair went up on my back, I turned around and could see something black in the quaking aspen coming our way.

My horse was going around in a circle and jerked loose, and away he went. All I could see of Ole and the horses was a big cloud of snow they had kicked up. I thought . . . good hell, my only weapon is my meat axe. I turned around to see how close Old Grizz was and there, just outside of the trees, stood this big old bull moose looking at me like I was crazy.

Well, I'll tell you, I walked a half mile before my legs stopped shaking and another mile before I stopped looking over my shoulder. Then, up the trail came Ole leading my horse and he was still stuttering. He wanted to know, "H-h-how I got aw-aw-aw-away from the Gr-gr-grizzly?" "Well," I said, "I'll tell you. When he came out of the timber after me it scared the crap out of me; he slipped in it and broke his neck. That's how I out ran him, but I still couldn't run fast enough to catch you!" Then Ole started laughing and I joined him. We got the pack horses and went to camp telling jokes to each other about "Old Grizz."

Sweaty Saddle Blankets

Hunting areas in Wyoming open and close at different times, depending on game populations, hunting pressure and migration. Some of the elk that spend the summers in Yellowstone migrate to the Jackson feed ground late in the year, depending on the snowfall, but usually around October 15th through November, and they come in different herds and at different times. The area our camp was in closed the fifteenth of November, so by the twentieth we had our camp torn down and packed out. We were putting the gear away for the winter when my old friend from town, Fritz Stevens, stopped by.

We had been talking about going hunting together for a few years. Fritz said that he hadn't gone hunting this year because they had been too busy at the sawmill. He was a sawyer for the sawmill in Dubois and is one of those kind who doesn't miss a day's work. He had spent most of his life working in the woods, back in the days when they skidded timber and moved the sawmills with horses.

I hadn't filled my elk permit yet, either. When you are guiding, sometimes you don't get the chance; then, you have to take a few days to hunt for yourself. So I told Fritz maybe we should go on the other side, down in Red Creek where it was still open. I had hunted this country before and had had good luck.

This time of year you had to fight snow to get in there, but we decided to give it a try. Fritz had to work half a day the next day, then he had two days off as it was Thanksgiving. At noon the next day we loaded up six of the strongest horses on the ranch. I knew that we would have to break through some deep snow to get over the top; then we put in our horse feed, grub, and bedrolls. There were loggers up Sheridan Creek who had the road plowed open, so we drove to the end of the road and parked the truck in a turn-around. The snow was too deep to get off the road, and we knew the loggers were not going to be using the road until Monday. We unloaded the horses and put our gear on the pack horse, then had a handful of granola and started off.

We had about eight miles to go and four of that to get to the top. Snow was about eight inches deep and was hard on the horses; we had to keep trading horses to break the trail. I had a big sorrel horse we called Tiny Tim, he was about sixteen hands high , well-built, and had a lot of "go" to him. When we got within a mile of the top, the snow got deeper and was up to the horses' bellies. We came out of the timber in a big meadow. The horse I was riding was just about played out so I changed horses and saddled Tiny Tim.

The wind had blown the snow and made this meadow look level, but I knew better. I had been across it before and knew there was a creek about in the middle. We started across. I could feel the power in Tiny Tim that the other horse had been lacking. The snow was a lot deeper than I was expecting. There was a trail across the meadow, but the snow had covered all signs. The wind was causing a little ground blizzard. I couldn't look into the wind long because the blowing snow hurt my face.

I knew we were close to the creek when, all of a sudden, down into the snow we went. My horse's head was completely under the snow, and the only thing that was out of the snow was my shoulder and head. The old horse started lunging so I started grabbing leather as if I were riding a bronc. I knew we were down in the creek, but Tiny Tim was still on his feet. He had broken through the ice and I could hear the splashing of water when I felt him go down to his knees, and we were both completely buried in the snow.

I couldn't see anything! I thought about getting off, but with both of us under the snow, neither one of us could see. Chances were I would end up underneath him and get stepped on or tromped, so I decided to just hang on and stay aboard. This old horse was not a quitter—he had a heart and the strength to go with it.

I knew the only way out was for him to get up on his feet and start scratching his way out. I remembered that the bank was about a foot high. Somehow, with me on his back, he got up and kept lunging until we got out. Then, he kept going until I had to stop him. It must have felt good to have snow only up to his belly after going through that.

We had turned the pack horses loose and they were right on my trail. The five horses broke a good trail for Fritz. Lucky thing the snow was still powder, if it would have been crusted I don't think we would have gotten through.

By the time we crossed over the top and got down into Squaw Creek it was dark. A couple more miles brought us to Triangle C's old hunting camp. We thought this was as good a place as any to bed down for the night. The snow here was a foot deep. I knew there was a spring for drinking water, and I thought there would be a pile of wood. So we unsaddled the horses and tried to give them a drink of water, but the spring and creek were frozen over and had a good foot of snow on top of them. We didn't have the tools to get to the water, so we tied the horses up and gave them some hay pellets and grain for the night.

We tried to find the woodpile but it must have been buried in the snow. Therefore we had another couple handfuls of granola and ate a little snow for water. Then we got the bedrolls out, and damned if we hadn't left one bedroll at the barn when we were getting things loaded. Fritz thought I got it and, of course, I thought he did. It was cold, about ten below, so we got all the sweaty saddle blankets and pads, laid them down on the snow, and then we laid on them and covered up with the bedroll. It damn sure was a long night. We didn't take off any clothes, not even our hats or gloves. It wasn't the cold that kept me awake, but the smell of those sweaty horse pads was hell. I could smell them all night. But daylight finally came.

Before we had left, I had told Fritz to get something to eat for breakfast that would not take much time and didn't have to be cooked, because we were only going to stay overnight and the next day. So he got a bag of granola. I was to get the stuff for lunch and supper, so I brought a sandwich, tea bags, and a big sack of granola! We hadn't known we would each bring the same thing, but we wound up with plenty of granola. So that's what we ate for breakfast—granola and a handful of snow. By morning the horses hadn't eaten all their feed because they were too thirsty.

We saddled up and started riding down towards Red Creek. Back then there were no roads in this country. Since then, the timber outfits have timbered out some of the country and put in a good road that goes right down Red Creek and over Squaw Creek. The closer we got to Red Creek, the less snow there was, and we started seeing elk. The first herd we saw had about thirty head in it. There was a lot of open country down where Squaw Creek comes into Red Creek, and all the elk seemed to be out in the open and out of range. There were a couple of nice bulls in that herd, and from this spot we could see four different herds, all of them out of range.

The elk had migrated into this area and would stay until the snow pushed them down. It was only about twenty miles to the feed ground from here. We rode on down and were just about to cross Red Creek when, up on the other side, a herd of elk started coming out of a patch of timber and crossing the big sagebrush opening. But they were all out of range. This was the biggest herd I had ever seen except on the feed ground.

We got off the horses and tried to count how many were in the herd. I counted about 200 head and Fritz counted around 300. There were about fifteen or twenty mature bulls and a hell of a lot of smaller ones. They just kept coming. We sat there and counted for an hour before they finally all got across. It was all open between them and us, so we could not come up on them. That was one of the most beautiful sights I·have ever seen while hunting.

We got on the horses and rode off in that direction. We hadn't gone far when we came upon a log cabin—an old cow camp nestled in a patch of timber. It had a sod roof with a big seven-point bull elk skull and an old buffalo skull hanging on it. Fritz and I both remarked that if they had any kind of a road into this country that those skulls would not last the first day. That was the last cabin I have seen that people had not molested.

This cabin reminded me of when I was a kid. My mother's family were all sheep people, and my uncle had built an old log cabin. He always left food in it with a note that read, "Please make yourself at home, eat what you want, and use my bunk. But, please clean up, and leave the cabin like you found it." And folks always did. Almost everytime, if they had eaten food they would leave money. I hate to say this, but it's a dog sad, different kind of world today. It breaks my heart to think that my grandchildren won't see how people used to respect each other and their property.

We got the horses and ourselves a good drink, put the horses in the corral by the cabin and gave them a feeding of grain. We went in the cabin and built a good fire, had some granola and boiled water for tea. It sure felt good to thaw out and have something hot to drink. The bad part about the heat was that it made us smell like old work horses from sleeping on those sweaty horse pads and blankets.

We decided to leave the pack horses in the corral, take the saddle horses and go hunting. We hadn't been gone but an hour when we were in a big patch of timber. All of a sudden there were elk all around us and runnning in different directions. Most of them didn't know where we were—they were just running because the others had spooked them. Fritz and I got off our horses and got our rifles out. One big bull stopped under a pine tree and looked at us. I told Fritz to shoot him. He was looking right at him but could not see him until he took off running. The timber was so thick that Fritz didn't get a shot off.

Well, before it was all over we both wound up with spikes. We had just

109

seen more mature bulls that day than most people see in a lifetime, but we each just got a spike. By the time we got them cleaned, quartered, and loaded on the pack horses it was dark, and we had a hell of a long ride ahead of us. We just turned the pack horses loose so they could find their way through the rough spots and we started working our way home.

The only bad place was coming out of Squaw Creek. The trail was icy in a couple of spots, and we had to get off and lead the horses so they would not slip and go down. The moon came out and you could almost see as well as if it were daylight. We could see the trail we made coming in, and so it wasn't bad traveling.

When we came to where Tiny Tim and I had all that fun getting buried in snow, I was a little concerned, but we went right through without any trouble at all. We got back to the truck about midnight, loaded the horses and gear and then drove to the ranch. We unloaded the horses, unsaddled them and put the gear away, then fed and turned the horses loose. By the time we got the elk hung up it was three in the morning.

Then we went up to the ranch house and had a hot cup of coffee. Fritz said to me, "You have to be crazy to go through what we just did and call it *fun*, but I sure had a good time . . . even though we worked like horses, and didn't get much sleep. When we did, we slept on sweaty saddle blankets and still smelled like a horse. We ate granola for two days which is like eating horse feed, and when I went to the bathroom it looked like a horse had been there." We both got a big laugh out of that. Then he stood up and whinnied at me and said, "I know I look like I've been *rode hard and put away wet*, but I'm going home to my horse stall and bed down for the night!"

110

Bugling Elk #1

B ugling an elk has to be one of the biggest thrills of hunting. I remember one time I had a hunter by the name of Ken, and this was the third time we were hunting together. The year before he had gotten a nice six-point bull elk. At that time we were hunting out of the hunting camp, which was twelve miles back in on horseback. He was now sixty-four years old and thought that this year it might be better if he hunted out of the ranch, instead of riding in that twelve miles and living in a tent.

I just happened to know of a spot where there were usually elk in the area of the ranch. It was a pretty good horse ride from the ranch, on the other side of the Pinnacles. The best way to get in there was over Bonneville Pass. This area was not hunted too hard in those days, and there were quite a few elk that would drift in there through the summer and feed in the meadows under the cliffs. Quite often through the fly season they would spend their days out on top where there was always a good breeze blowing that would help keep the flies off them, and they would feed on that high-protein mountain grass. By hunting season they would be nice and fat.

The first morning we trucked the horses to the end of the road at daylight. Then we started riding back into those little meadows, and by noon Ken had gotten a shot at a nice bull but had missed him. After that we stopped at the edge of a meadow, unsaddled the horses and had lunch. The sun was warm, so after we got through eating, we took a nap.

I woke up with the sound of Ken trying to get his rifle out. I looked around, and on the other side of the meadow were some elk standing just inside the trees watching us. By the time Ken got his rifle, they had disappeared like smoke in the woods. Ken said that he had heard this funny high-pitched squealing sound, raised up and looked around, and there at the edge of the meadow were the elk with a nice bull among them. I told him that the squealing sound must have been the bull. Ken had never heard the sound of a bugling elk before, and he thought it was a coyote or something.

We sat and visited awhile, then decided to ride up to these little pockets under the cliffs. There is about a half a dozen of these small meadows separated by little patches of timber. By the time we rode up to the first one it was getting late as it had taken us longer to ride up there than I had figured. Before we rode into each meadow we would get off the horses and walk to the edge of the timber, look it over, than stand there for ten or fifteen minutes before going on. At the fourth meadow we got off the horses and walked to the edge of it. We were standing behind some trees watching the meadow, when all of a sudden a cow elk walked out of the timber on the other side and started feeding. She'd raise her head, stick her nose in the air, and try to pick up scent. A few minutes later out came another cow and two calves. Behind them, back in the timber, a bull let out a couple of squeals, then we could hear him raking his horns up and down on a tree.

I told Ken, "Let's get down behind this log, and I'll try to bugle him out. If he does come out, wait until you can get a good shot before moving, because the bull will know from the sound of me bugling right where we are and will be looking in our direction." So we quietly slipped behind the big log, so as not to spook the cows, then I picked up a stick about two inches thick and about a foot and a half long. In front if me was a perfect little tree about six inches thick. I broke off some of the branches vigorously, making quite a bit of noise doing it, like the elk do. Then I raked the tree with the stick three or four times, up and down with strokes of about two feet long. Then with my mouth I sucked in air really hard making sounds like a bull squealing, trailing it off with a couple grunts. I didn't have time to repeat it when the bull answered with a thrilling, high-pitched squeal, raking his horns again. The sound of it raised the hair on my back; from all the noise he was making, you could tell he was on the fight. We could hear him crashing through the timber, breaking brush, then into the meadow he came on a dead run heading right for us. Within a second or two he was half-way across the meadow and was within fifty to seventy-five yards of us.

The thrill and excitement was so great, Ken froze in place, so I grabbed his shoulder and shook him and said, "You'd better try it now." He stood up and the bull came to a sliding stop. They just stood there looking at each other like they were hypnotized for a second. Then Ken said, "My

112

God!" and just stood there looking at that bull with his arms hanging down to his knees, his rifle in his hands, and kept saying, "My God, oh my God." Then the bull whirled around and laid his massive horns back, opened his mouth and was gone.

What a sight! It all happened so fast that even I was shook up and had to lean back against the tree and and take a deep breath! Ken was still standing there looking in the direction where the bull had disappeared in the timber still saying, "My God," and had never raised his rifle above his knees, looking like he had been thunderstruck. I said, "Ken are you all right?" After looking at him for a second, I had to laugh. He looked at me and smiled a little, then I think he started to come out of it. He took off his hat, scratched his head and said, "You know, I got so excited because he was so magnificent, that I forgot to shoot!" We both laughed.

It was almost dark, and we had five miles of horse riding ahead of us. By the time we rode out, loaded the horses and drove back to the ranch it was almost midnight.

A few months later I got a phone call from Ken. After we had said our howdys and all, he said, "Bugling that elk up to us is the biggest thrill I ever had hunting and even though I didn't get him, I will cherish that moment the rest of my life!"

© gary shoop

Bugling Elk #2

Back in the early sixties before I changed my home range, I lived in Montana. A friend of mine, Bill, and I were hunting elk up near the Bob Marsh Wilderness Area around the first week of September. Neither one of us had hunted in this part of the country before and had no idea just where the elk would be hanging out. We had three pack horses with us in case we did find one. Other than that, we were traveling light with mostly dehydrated foods. We figured part of our diet would be ruffed grouse which were quite plentiful in this country in those days and they sure were good grub. We usually cooked them over an open fire by turning them over and over on a green stick. We would rub them with butter and sprinkle them with a little salt and pepper and cook them until they were golden brown.

Anyway, we both had hunted elk enough to know that when you don't know the country, and if you have enough horse flesh, the best way to find them is to move camp with you on a pack horse as you hunt until you find where they are. We had been riding all day and it was getting towards evening when we came out on a point at the top of a canyon called Denim Creek. We glassed the canyon with our field glasses and spotted a small herd of elk with a nice bull among them. We studied the layout of the canyon and tried to figure out the best way to get to the bottom. It looked like it wouldn't be too bad traveling with horses, but when we got down in there, we found out that the nice traveling look was just the top side.

By night time we were in the bottom and had set up camp. We no sooner had finished feeding and staking out the the horses, when below camp an old bull began bugling. Then off to the side of us one answered, and not long after, one above us started squealing, so I decided to have a little fun. I let out a few grunts and squeals. This seemed to get the bull above camp a little excited and he started moving off the mountain in our direction. Within about ten minutes it sounded like he was getting quite close. All of a sudden, off to our left in the timber, another bull started squealing. It was quite dark by this time, so we lay on the ground. From there we could see the outline of the horses, and they all had their heads up and were looking in the direction of the bugling.

Suddenly we could hear the elk clashing horns together, the sound echoing through the canyon. In a few minutes they moved out of the timber and into the meadow where the horses were. We could make them out by the sky light. They were so close we could hear them blowing and grunting as they clashed horns. Below camp we could hear three or four other bulls still bugling. The canyon was alive with their sound.

As I lay there listening to that beautiful wild sound all around us and at the same time seeing those two magnificent bulls fighting in their natural habitat, it sent chills through me and made the hair on the back of my neck stand up. I could not help but feel how lucky I was to be able to live in this country and be fortunate enough to see this. One of the horses whinnied just then and spooked the elk, and they disappeared into the trees. From all that excitement I couldn't get much sleep that night. Every time I'd doze off, I'd dream about those bulls and wake myself up.

We did not start a fire to fix breakfast that morning because we did not want the smoke to drift through the canyon and spook the elk, so we ate crackers and cold stew. We took a small lunch and left camp on foot. Then we heard a bull bugling below camp. It sounded like he was about in the same place that we heard some last night, so we worked our way down there, taking our time and being as quiet as possible. As long as we could hear him squealing now and then, I thought we would just keep moving in his direction. There was a little breeze blowing up the canyon in our favor. We kept working our way down there until it sounded like the bull was only a block away.

The trees had thinned out some, and there was a little opening, but we still could not see him. I figured this was about as close as we could get without spooking him off, so I picked up a stick and raked it up and down on a tree like elk do with their horns. With my mouth I started sucking in air and making squealing sounds like an old bull. Then we sat there very quietly and waited. We heard the bull walking in our direction so I let out a short little grunt, then raked the tree vigorously. That got him excited, and he started toward us. Just as his head came through the brush, Bill made a clean shot. He was a nice fat five-point and would make good chewing for us through the winter.

Bugling Elk #3

A few years ago, a couple friends of mine, Wilbur Keas and John Randolph, and I went hunting up Caldwell Creek. None of us had ever hunted in this area before. It was the ninth of October; the weather was chilly and there was a skiff of snow on the ground.

The first morning we left the horses in camp, split up, and went hunting on foot in different directions. We all had either heard or seen elk that morning, but by noon none of us had gotten one. By the time I got back to camp, John and Wilbur were already there.

We visited awhile and had lunch. John asked where I thought would be a good place to hunt that evening. I had to ponder on that a spell because this was not my home range. I answered, "Probably one direction is just as good as the next, but I've got one of those bright, teenage cowboy ideas. I think I'll ride up Caldwell 'til I come to timberline and see what's up there, and you can sure come along if you'd like too." Wilbur said he thought he would just as soon hunt on foot in the same area he had hunted that morning. John decided to come with me.

We saddled our horses, took our time and worked our way up Caldwell. Just short of timberline we found a good place to sit and watch at the edge of an opening, and there was a lot of elk sign. John said he'd sit there until dark, so I left and rode on.

There was a little wind blowing and in this canyon the sun disappears behind the mountain an hour earlier than it does out in the open so it was getting damned cold. I took my jacket out from behind the saddle and put it on. I found another opening and watched it until almost dark. By then my feet were getting cold from not moving around, so I decided to go back down, pick up John, and go back to camp.

When I got back to where John was, he was still sitting in the same spot. He was so cold that he could hardly talk through his chattering teeth. I thought to myself that this man has got to be tough to sit in one spot all this time as cold as it was. He said, "Well, I'd better go get my horse." He got up and started walking over the hill. His leg joints were kind of frozen up from sitting on that cold mountain for so long that it caused him to walk like an old-time cowman who had spent too much time in the saddle. You can always pick out an old cowboy from a herd: his legs are stiff, his ankles bend front and back as his knees bend sideways, and his hips are solid from spending too much time in the saddle and nights on the ground. John was walking just that way from being so cold. While I was waiting for him I thought I would do a little bugle practicing. I let out an elk squeal and sat there on my horse until John came back.

We started to ride off when I saw this bull across the canyon coming out of the quaking aspen. John got off his horse and took a shot at him. It looked like he might have hit him, but he ran back into the trees. By the time we got over there it was dark, so we decided to come back early in the morning and see if we could pick up his tracks. We went back to camp to get thawed out.

The next morning we ate and were on the horses just before daylight. We had been riding for about forty-five minutes and were in a thick patch of timber. The trail was frozen and the horses were making quite a bit of noise. All of a sudden, down in the timber below us, this bull bugled. I stopped, and with my mouth I answered him by sucking in air and squealing, trailing off with a couple of grunts. I hadn't quite finished when the bull answered back, and by the sound he must have been on the fight and coming our way. John had never bugled elk up before and did not savvy what was going on.

I jumped off the horse and ran down into the timber to get away from the horses. I knew the bull would know right where the horses were from my bugling, and I wanted to get away from them so he would be looking for them, not me. He was grunting and squealing with every step. When he got within a few hundred yards he stopped. I waited a few minutes, then I let out a loud high-pitched squeal and raked a tree with a stick. That got him on the fight again, and within a minute he was right in front of me. The wind was in my favor, and I could see his horns and part of his body. He started to circle me and walked through a small opening between two trees when I bagged him. He was a nice six-point—big and fat.

All this time, which was really only a few minutes, John sat on his horse wondering what the hell I was doing. He brought my saddle horse down so I could get my axe and saw to quarter him. When John saw how big he was, he said that it was really a thrill, even though he did not know what was happening. That was just one of those times that a bull in the rut got excited from the sound of horses and thought they were elk.

I have bugled quite a few elk up to me through the years, and a few hunters have bagged them because of it. I don't want you to get the idea that I am any kind of an expert at it, because I am not, but I have had fun doing it and would like to explain some of the methods I have used.

If you can catch a mature bull when he is really in the rut, he will answer to about any kind of a squealing sound. After all, elk are like people—they don't all sound the same. I have heard elk answer coyotes and even mules. If you are serious about bugling one up, the first thing you should do is get downwind of him because an elk has a terrific nose and knows how to use it. When the wind is in my favor, I like to make sounds that resemble a bull raking his horns on a tree. I get a stick about a foot and a half long and about two inches thick. Then if I figure he is close enough to hear me, I will pick a tree that is about four to six inches thick, break some of the branches off, making noise as I break them, then rake the stick up and down on the tree with strokes of about a foot to two feet in length. I usually bugle with my mouth and that takes some practice. I don't blow out to do it, instead I suck in air.

The best store-bought elk bugle that I've found is made by a man by the name of Larry Jones from Oregon. It looks like the old radiator hose that has the wire coil in it. It is about a foot long and has a replacable reed in one end. This bugle really sounds like an elk and reaches out a long distance.

After I get a bull coming in, I don't like to bugle too much. If you try to bugle a bull across an opening, usually he will circle it instead of exposing himself going through it. Lots of times, even though you have the wind in your favor, when he gets close he will circle you, pick up your scent, and you will never see him.

If I hear a bull bugling a long way off, and I want to try to bugle him up, I'll work my way closer to him before I start, because it seems like the closer you are the more excited he gets. He thinks the other bull is coming in to take his harem away and he'll get on the fight a lot easier than if you are far away. I have bugled and had a bull answer me many times but not come in. But there have been times when it has snowed a little, or the weather has turned cold, or it is just getting daylight or dark that I have called up two or three bulls, one right after another. I'll tell you what pard, it is well worth the time and effort to try, because once you've called one up to you, you're hooked for life!

118

Scar-Face, the Horse

We needed a few more horses for hunting, pack trips, and trail rides, so I decided to go to a horse sale. I got there a couple of hours early and went out into the corrals to look the horses over. That's when I saw this horse with a big scar on his face. The scar ran from his left ear down under his right eye. You could see where they had sewn him up; it looked like it must have been a deep, bad cut. Other than that he was a big horse—good muscle and wide between the eyes.

I climbed into the corral full of horses and walked right up to him, rubbed him down, and picked up all four feet. He looked like he was a cross between a quarterhorse and a thoroughbred. I kind of took a liking to him. I bridled him and led him around the corral. I took off my hat and waved it at him. He didn't seem to mind at all. Then I got on and rode him around the corral. He seemed to be well broken.

When I got down I saw an elderly gentleman standing outside the corral watching me. He said it was his horse and had belonged to his son, Bob. When the horse was three years old, his boy was at a friend's house practicing roping. They had dug a posthole outside of the arena, and then, to keep someone from stepping into it they put an iron pipe in the hole. The iron pipe had fallen towards the arena fence and was sticking through to the inside. Bob was on his horse and just about to rope a calf when the horse hit the pipe head first and that's how he got the scar. I could see tears in the old man's eyes.

I asked him if he was all right and he said, "Well, it just made me think of my boy. Two years later he joined the Marines and went to Vietnam. He never came back. No one had ridden the horse since then until just now when you did." I'll tell you what, I could hardly speak at all. He was the nicest looking guy and had the saddest face.

I asked him how much he wanted for the horse. He said he didn't know,

© Gary Shoop

that he was going to run him through the auction ring and whatever money he brought would be fine. I looked at the auction number on the horse, it was 182. That meant he would be one of the last horses through the ring, and by that time, the only buyers left would be horse traders. I knew he would not get a good price that late in the day so I said, "You tell me what you want for him and I will buy him." He gave me a price and I bought him.

He said to me, "I hope you aren't buying the horse because of what I just told you." I shook my head and said, "No, I just bought myself one damn good saddle horse and I think it's the buy of the night." Then I told him I would take good care of that old pony, and we shook hands and said goodbye. I've never seen him again, but I will always remember him.

We bought a truckload of horses, and they all looked like good horse flesh. When we got back home, I named the old horse Scar-Face. I used him around the ranch for a few days and he turned out to be a top horse.

I had to clear some trails that went into some lakes where we took people for overnight horse rides, so I went out and caught old Scar-Face and a pack horse. I saddled them up, got the axe, a chain saw, and a big lunch and took off. The trail had a lot of downfall in it and took more time than I expected to get it cleared. I worked right up until dark, then I put the gear on the pack horse and started back. I was a little worried about Scar-Face not being able to find his way in the dark. There were some real bad places where the trail cut along the side of a cliff and had steep drop-offs. Old Scar-Face put his nose within a couple of inches of

120

the ground, and, I think, he must have stepped in his own tracks all the way back to the ranch. This horse was proving to be one fine pony. You could catch him any place; he could find his way at night; he was sure-footed, strong, easy riding, and good natured; he handled extra well; and he was a good looking horse except for the scar on his face.

When hunting season came I rode Scar-Face to guide. I had three horses that I used through hunting season, which lasted for a good two and a half months. I used a fresh horse every day. Some days were long and hard on a horse; we hunted in some pretty rough and damn steep country.

One of the other horses was a palomino I called "Golden Boy." He was a well-bred horse; they said his daddy came from the King Ranch in Texas. Some horse rancher bought him in Texas and brought him back to his ranch in Idaho. This rancher had a young man working for him by the name of Dick. Dick had a range mare and one day, when no one was at the ranch, he put his mare in with the stud from Texas. That colt was the horse I called "Golden Boy".

They started breaking him at three and got him coming along fine but had to turn him out to pasture for winter. Then Dick got interested in cars and women and forgot about the horse. A couple of years later they rounded up a bunch of horses, and the yellow horse was in the string. He was five years old then. They cut him out and put him in a corral by himself, but when Dick tried to ride him, he got thrown sky high. Then, one by one, the same thing happened to all of his friends. For sure, none of them were much of a hand with a horse.

Dick traded that yellow horse to his cousin and I bought him for $80.00. I liked the way he looked; he was put together right, but, man oh man, was he snorty. I put him in the pasture, and he ran to the other side with his tail up in the air. A few days later I got him into a corral and started breaking him. First I put a saddle on him, and he bucked like a salted dog. Then I sacked him out with a piece of plastic. "Sacking him out" means waving a rag or piece of plastic all over and around him until he stops jumping and pays no attention to it. After that I slipped on to him and away we went. He bucked around the corral until he was covered with white lather, stopped and caught his breath, and started bucking again. I held his head up so he couldn't buck as hard, but he still bucked. I rode him everyday for two months and every monring when I got on him, he would squeal and buck!

It got so that every morning the guests at the ranch would come down to the corrals to see if he was going to throw me, and he succeeded in doing it a few times. One morning when I got up I was so sore from

121

riding him that I told my wife, "If that yellow devil bucks this morning, I'm going to trade him off to a bucking string." So, I went down to the corrals and saddled him up, got on, and he didn't buck, nor has he bucked with me since, although he has thrown a stranger or two.

The third horse that I rode was a horse called "Dan" that we were just starting to break. He was a big, gentle range horse, sorrel in color, and not a bad looker. After riding Golden Boy and Scar-Face he seemed a little docile, but he had the right kind of makings for a dude horse. Before hunting season was over he got so gentle and slow that I had some of the hunters riding him.

After riding Scar-Face and Golden Boy all season, if I had to choose between them it would be hard to tell which one was the best pony. At one time I thought I would never like a horse as much as Golden Boy, but I think I like Scar-Face almost as well.

The last day of hunting season finally came. There was quite a bit of snow on the ground, and it was cold as hell. The last hunters had a successful hunt; they all filled out except two. After getting their meat and gear packed, we rode out. In a couple of places the trail was iced up and slicker than a greased pig. We had the hunters get off while we led their horses through the slick spots. We got them back to the ranch and all that was left was to go back and break camp and pack it out. Breaking camp in late November is not a job for milk maids. It's a cold, miserable job that takes long hours. It took twenty pack horses and three men to get our camp out in one trip. We left the ranch early in the morning; it had turned bitter cold the last couple of days.

We got all the horses saddled up, and over Randolph Mountain we went. On the other side the north slopes are covered with black timber and springs. The springs were iced up and made for dangerous traveling. The horses had a hard time standing up in places. At Lava Creek the water was only open in the middle, and the snow was just about up to the horses' knees. It was real hard going. I rode Golden Boy in and turned Scar-Face loose. We got into camp about three in the afternoon. The horses were unsaddled, hobbled, and fed and then we got a good, warm fire going in the cook tent. After supper we went to bed, only to get up before daylight. We rustled up some breakfast and went back to breaking camp.

There were six sleeping tents, two saddle tents, one grain tent, and a big Army cook tent that comes apart in two pieces. Just the cook tent alone took two of our biggest horses to carry it. The tents weighed forty to sixty pounds more than usual because they had ice frozen on them a foot above where they had been touching the ground. All the snow that

122

was piled on top of the tents would slide off and build up on the sides and turn to ice. When we pulled the tents down, we had to be careful not to rip them. We couldn't get all the ice off, so they'd just get put away until next spring when it warmed up.

We left one tent up with just enough grub for us to eat until we got the whole camp packed. We filled and weighed all the panniers and put the top packs, with each set of panniers, in individual piles. This took all day, so with the lanterns we saddled all the pack horses. I had to use Scar-Face for a pack horse. Saddling twenty head of pack horses takes a few hours, so we got a couple of hours of sleep before it was time to get up and at it again.

We were up before daylight, had breakfast, and then tore down the last tent, packed it up and started packing all of the gear on the horses. When we finally came to the last of the twenty pack horses it was getting late.

I took the lead, and we started down the trail. Slim got in the middle and Bob brought up the rear. With twenty head of pack horses strung out, only on a big, long meadow could you see them all.

The day must have been around zero degrees. Everything was going fine until we came to Lava Creek. At this particular spot, Lava Creek ran up against the mountain and was in the pines where the sun never hits at that time of year. There was only about a foot of water that was open in the middle of the creek, and going out of Lava Creek on the other side was a steep bank. I broke through the ice first and crossed with all the horses right behind me. They knew they were headed home and wanted to keep on moving. When they came up out of the water onto the steep bank they were splashing water, and the bank turned to ice. Only three or four of them got through and then they started slipping and falling down.

One of the horses slipped backwards into Scar-Face while Scar-Face was trying to get up the bank and caused him to slide back into the water. He went under the ice and floundered and kicked until he finally got up on his feet. By then, I was off my horse and, with a rope, was stopping the horses from coming up the icy bank. I was turning them downstream, letting them drift down and find different spots to get out of the creek. At each spot they found, only four or five horses could get up the bank before it turned to ice. Again, I'd holler and whack them across the nose with the rope to turn them downstream to another spot.

Old Slim was at the first crossing, stopping the horses from coming out of the steep, icy bank and turning them downstream towards me. Finally, we got all the horses out of the stream except old Scar-Face. He was standing in the middle of the creek humped up and white from the ice on him. I jumped on my horse and went out and put a rope around his neck and pulled him to the bank.

By this time the pack horses were going up the trail for home and scattered in every direction. I hollered at Slim and asked him to turn the horses back down while Bob and I changed packs. We had picked up the loose pack horses along the way and started taking the pack off Scar-Face. It was so cold that the knots on the ropes were frozen. We had to use pliers to get them untied.

We finally got the pack off Scar-Face and onto the other horse. Poor old Scar-Face walked up the trail. I could see the icicles hanging on his belly and chin and he was still white from the ice. *You know, a horse can't tell you how bad he hurts or where, he just endures and tries to go on.*

By now, Slim had pushed some of the horses back down to us. The pack horses were getting tired and ornery and were starting to fight. It was dark and damn cold and we were getting cold, hungry, and tired, too. We couldn't see all the horses as they were going in all directions. I asked Slim to bring up the rear and check for stray horses.

We finally got over the mountain and down to the truck. By the time we got the horses unpacked and put in the corrals and fed it was two in the morning. It was about that time I noticed that I hadn't seen Scar-Face. I asked Bob and Slim if they had seen him. They couldn't remember seeing him and we were dog-tired and needed some sleep. We drove to the ranch and ate and then went to bed.

The next morning we went back to get the horses. Scar-Face was not in the corral with them. This got me to worrying. I had a bad feeling and knew there was something wrong. So I told Slim and Bob to take the horses back to the ranch and leave the pickup and horse trailer for me, and I would see if I could find Scar-Face. I saddled Golden Boy and went looking. I rode up and over Randolph Mountain and that's where I found him lying on the side of the trail, just about where I had last seen him.

I felt so bad. He was such an honest and good horse. I thought then if I had only taken a manny off a pack horse and wrapped it around him, he might have made it. I knew better, but just didn't think of it. Right then, I wished that someone would have been up there to give me a swift kick. I thought of the old man I bought him from and what he had said about his boy, Bob, who had trained such a good horse.

Every time I went down that trail and passed his bones I got a lump in my throat. I do believe that over the Great Divide, if there are greener pastures and cold, sweet mountain water, that is where you can find old Scar-Face.

124

Chico

I would like to tell you a story about my little girl's horse, Chico. Chico was a mare, blood chestnut in color. We got her from a friend of ours, Carl Boulden. He had raised her from a baby and he thought the world of her. This little mare was real quick on her feet—she could spin on a dime and give you a nickel change. She was out of an old range mare and a quarterhorse stud. Chico was a pleasant-looking horse with good muscle and a kind head.

Karrie and Chico seemed to match each other right from the start. I think they fell in love the first day. Karrie would ride her around the yard with nothing but a halter, and in the corral she would ride her with nothing at all. Then she'd lie on her back and put her arms around her neck and talk to her.

All three of my kids used to ride Chico and play games on her, like pushing each other off, and she would just stand there like nothing was happening. When Chico would see Karrie coming home from school, she would run up to the fence for attention. That horse seemed to be at ease when Karrie was around. She seemed to have a little human in her; she trusted Karrie and would do anything for her.

When Karrie started using her for barrel racing they won a bushel basket full of ribbons. Chico had a lot of heart and was as quick as a cat, but was as gentle as a lamb with my kids—the perfect babysitter. Her blood chestnut color made Karrie's long, blonde hair stand out and look so pretty when running through the barrels. We all felt that Chico was just part of the family, and we had her for five years.

I used to cut Christmas trees every year and sell them. One year my brother and I had been cutting for three days and had stacked up quite a pile. We cut in a canyon where the road only went up half-way, so we had to drag the trees down to where we could load them. If you drug them on the ground it would pull the needles off and skin the bark, so we would load them on car hoods and pull them behind the horses. We had been doing this for a couple of hours, and it was hard work on the horses. My brother was using Chico, and I had my old saddle horse.

I was up on the hill above my brother loading trees when I heard him holler. Just then I could hear tin banging on rocks. I looked down and could see Chico on a dead run. The hood was airborne right behind her. My brother had ridden her up to the pile of trees and, when he got off, he didn't think to tie her up, he just dropped the reins. Then he started throwing trees on the hood that was tied behind Chico. The weight of the trees made the hood move and slide into Chico's hind leg. This scared her and she jumped forward and jerked the hood after her. Chico took off on a dead run with the hood behind her. She was going so fast that the hood got airborne. When she saw that, it scared her so bad she started running for her life.

I ran off the hill to where my brother was and started tracking her until she came to a fence. The government had put the barbed wire fence in the year before. Chico turned and ran along side of it. I tracked her along the fence for a ways and then the fence went up a steep side hill. That's when she got her leg through the barbed wire and cut it almost off. It was horrifying! When I got up to her she was lying on the ground. She kept lifting her head and nickering at me. She was trying to get up but couldn't.

I bent over in pain and threw up. That was the only time in my life I cried over a horse. I felt helpless! There was nothing I could do for her. She just kept lifting her head and nickering.

I never will forget that. I just could not bring myself to shoot her. My eyes were blurry and I was shaking so bad that I could not pull the trigger. I started back to where my brother was and met him half-way. He was on our tracks and was coming to see what had happened. I told him that I knew it was an accident and just one of those things, but he would have to take the pistol and shoot her. She was in such pain and suffering so bad. I knew she would bleed to death in a short time, and there was no way to save her.

The hard part came when I got home and had to tell Karrie. She just sobbed and sobbed. It broke her little heart.

I have always thought that the outside of a horse was good for the inside of a kid's head, and, to my kids, Chico sure proved this to be true. I prefer a gelding for my saddle horse because they seem to be less trouble, but I'll tell you what, that little mare, Chico, will always be my family's favorite, and *my* favorite, horse.

126

© garyshoop

127

Mules

Back when I was a young boy, my father used to buy and sell mules. In those days there was a good market for them because they were used in the mines.

Dad was well-known in these parts for being a good horse trader. There was a family that lived out of town on a little farm. The road to their house was mostly all dirt and had big ruts in it. When it rained it got really slippery and you could not drive on it without getting stuck. You won't believe this, but this family's name was Butterballs, and there were twenty-three kids in the family!

One of the boys, Neb, was in my room at school. He had been held back a couple years and was the bully of the class. I remember how he used to brag about the damndest things, like how many kids there were in his family and how tough they all were, how rich they were, how good-looking he was, and about his brother, Clem, who had gone to dancing school. (Everyone knew Clem was a little retarded). Being the bully, none of us kids disagreed with him, at least not to his face.

Neb asked if I would tell my dad that they had a couple of mules they wanted to sell. They ran out of hay and couldn't feed their milk cow or the mules. For the last month they had been feeding them lettuce and bread from the garbage in the back of the grocery stores.

When I told Dad, he asked if I would like to go with him. I said, "I sure would." It was fascinating watching him buying and trading horses or mules. He always got boot, even if it was only a sack of grain, a chicken, or a goat.

Well, it was in the spring, and the road to their house was muddy, and we slipped off into the ruts and got stuck. I got out and pushed, got wet and muddy, but we finally made it. As I remember, it was getting towards evening when we got to their house, and in every window you could see two or three kids with their noses pushed up against the glass staring at us. Then Mr. Butterballs came outside with about ten of his kids following him and was looking at us as if they hadn't had company for quite a spell. He shook hands with my dad and talked for awhile. The kids kept pulling faces and sticking their tongues out at me, and, when their Dad was not looking, one of them would poke or shove me. Then he asked us to come in the house.

In the middle of the living room was a pot-bellied stove, and they had a fire going in it. I remember there were a couple of chickens on the table when we went through the kitchen, and not one of the kids, including Mr. Butterballs, paid them any attention. The chickens just kept picking food off the table. I was quite cold from being wet, so I tried to get up next to the stove, but there were two dogs lying next to it. One showed his teeth and growled at me, then he grabbed my pantleg and ripped a piece of it off. One of the kids grabbed a two-by-four that was lying on a chair and smacked him over the head with it. The dog yiped and ran in the other room with the other dog right on his tail. The kids pointed at my ripped pantleg and laughed like hell.

Mrs. Butterballs was sitting in her rocking chair next to the stove, sewing. The house had a funny odor to it and there were holes all over the walls. My dad and Mr. Butterballs started out for the corrals. I started out with them but Dad said to stay there and get warm. I said, "I would rather go with you." He said, "No, stay there." My father was not the kind you sassed, so I walked back to the stove. I thought I had better get next to Mrs. Butterballs so the kids would not poke me, but that old hound dog had come back in the room and layed next to her. He started growling at me, so I stayed on the other side of the stove. Well, the kids kept pulling faces and sticking their tongues out, then one laid down behind me and the other pushed me over him. I jumped up and was going to poke him in the nose. Just then his mother said to him, "Jim, you hadn't ought to pick on company that way, you hear?"

All of a sudden, I heard the damnedest noise, and out of the other room came this oversized kid. He made a big jump and landed in the middle of the room, then, with a grin that went from ear to ear, he looked around and started dancing. It had to be Clem!

Well, Clem tippy-toed around the room and kicked a hole in the wall. Then he would tippy-toe on his toes and spin around in a circle, take off across the room, jump in the air and click his heels and kick another hole in the wall. I thought to myself, good hell, I can't believe I'm seeing this. No one seemed to mind nor did they say a word to him.

Mrs. Butterballs just kept on rocking in her chair and sewing. She looked as content as an old milk cow on green grass. Well, this kid kept tippy-toeing around the room and, every now and then, kicked another hole in the wall. This went on for about ten minutes then it got to where no one was paying him much attention, so he danced over to where his little sister was sitting on a chair and kicked it out from under her. She hit the floor screaming and started crying. His mother stopped rocking, bent over and picked up the two-by-four that the kid had hit the dog with, shook it at Clem and said, "Clem, you shouldn't tease your sister that a-way. Now, be good, you hear?"

Clem smiled even bigger, then jumped in the air and clicked his heels, tippy-toed over to where his mother was sitting, jumped into the air and swung his right foot back and brought it forward as if to kick the chair out from under his mother but stopped within an inch of doing it. Then, Clem started laughing and said, "You thought I was going to kick your chair, didn't you, Ma?" Ma replied, "Don't be so sassy Clem, you hear?" Then he tippy-toed across the room and jumped into the air and kicked another hole in the wall. His mother went back to sewing and rocking. I'll tell you, the inside of this house looked like it had been bombed in the World War II from old Clem practicing his dancing in there. I'll say one thing about him . . . as big and clumsy as he looked, he sure could tippy-toe.

About then I could hear my dad and Mr. Butterballs out in the yard loading the mules. That's what I was waiting for. I wanted to get out of that house before one of those kids poked me in the nose or something. I started outside and all the kids started following me including that damn dog. He came right up next to my heels, and every time I took a step he would growl. I asked one of the kids to get him away from me, but he just looked at me and laughed and pointed at my ripped pantleg.

My dad had one mule in the truck, but the other one was giving them trouble; he did not want to load. We kids got up close to watch. Dad was in the back of the truck with the lead rope trying to lead the mules in. Mr. Butterballs picked up a club and whacked the mule across the hind-end, the mule brayed and jumped into the truck, and at the same time, squirted mule manure all over us kids and Mr. Butterballs. That mule could squirt dung clear across the yard. They had not fed them any hay for better than a month, just the lettuce and bread they had gotten from behind the grocery store, and I guess that diet had upset their systems because they both crapped like no mules I had ever seen before, and boy, did it smell!

My father looked at us with that mule dung splattered all over us then

130

131

pointed a finger at Mr. Butterballs and tried to say something, but busted out laughing, bent over and clapped his k. _es, and leaned back against the truck for support. Pointing at Mr. Butterballs with one finger and wiping the tears out of his eyes with the other hand, that's when the other mule let out a hee-haw and stuck his tail out and squirted mule dung all over my dad's back and splattered that damn dog square in the face. Some of it must have gotten in his eyes because he started yipping and running around in a circle, then headed for the house as fast as he could go and ran under the porch crying. When we left I could still hear him under the house crying.

The mule got Mr. Butterballs all over his face and in his hair. Dad and we kids really thought it was funny, but Mr. Butterballs was not laughing. He wiped the mule manure from his eyes, then coughed, choked, and spit four or five times. Then you could tell he was on the fight because he turned to us kids and said, "Stop that laughing, do you hear?" But he looked so funny with the green hair and face we couldn't stop, so he picked up the club that he had used on the mule and took after his kids. All fifteen or twenty of them ran for the house.

I thought my dad would never stop laughing. Mr. Butterballs came back only to get his money. I'm sure he would have rather gone in the house. On the way back he was still coughing and choking and cussing the hell out of those mules. Dad paid him and never stopped laughing the whole time. Mr. Butterballs said, "Those worthless long-eared jackasses! I'm damned glad I don't own them because, if I did, I would shoot them!"

Mr. Butterballs came up to Dad, having cooled down a little by this time, to say good-bye. We started to drive away, the driveway made a sharp right turn, and just as we were making it, one of the mules let out another hee-haw and squirted Mr. Butterballs again. He threw his hat on the ground and jumped up and down on it like a mad brahma and cussed like I had never heard cussing before. We could see him in the mirror, and my dad got to laughing so hard, he had to stop the truck.

By the time we got the mules home, the back of that old truck looked like we had gotten a first-class paint job, it was bright green from the mule manure and looked kind of pretty but smelled like a coyote's den!

Hard Saddles and Sore Hind Ends

It was Friday morning, September 8, when I got a call telling me that two of the hunters were flying in and they would be landing about noon that day. I was to go pick them up and bring them back to the ranch.

The airport in Dubois was too small for commercial planes, so they were coming in their own plane. The runway is up on a hill above the Wind River and has some damn rough mountains on both sides. On the south is the Wind River Range and off to the north are the Absaroka Mountains with the Tetons to the west. If the weather is very rough you cannot land a plane. Earlier that morning it had been quite rough but had cleared off and had been nice for the past couple of hours. I got there about a half hour before the hunters landed. They came in, made a good landing, taxied up the runway, and parked.

When I drove up to the plane to give them a hand, they introduced themselves. The pilot's name was Bill, and his partner's name was Mike. Mike was a big man and an ex-football player. Mike had a camera around his neck and by now had taken a dozen pictures of everything. After the introductions, we got the gear out of the plane. There were a hell of a lot of cameras and gear. Mike was a professional photographer. They were both from Florida and had been good friends for many years.

We put all the stuff in the pickup and started back to the ranch. Driving back, Mike shot a roll of film through the window. When we got there, he asked if we could get all that camera paraphernalia on a pack horse and into camp without breaking it. I said, "It is possible." Mike asked if I could get him a horse that obeyed and would leave the other horses without giving any trouble so he could take pictures of the pack horses and of us riding. I thought I had just the horse for him.

The next morning after breakfast, we drove over the mountain to where the horses were. It took an extra hour to pack all the camera and gear because I wanted to make sure that none of it got broken, so I put it on a couple of the gentlest pack horses and cushioned the hell out of it. There were six hunters, three guides, one cook, and one horse wrangler.

Bill and Mike were my hunters. I had old Snake Eye saddled just for Mike and old Moose for Bill. Snake Eye had two glassy eyes with white rings on the outer pupils, and when he rolled his eyes, that white ring would look like a camera lens blinking on and off. He had an extra large head and a Roman nose and was raw-boned, big, and stout. When he was turned loose, if you found old Moose you found Snake Eye. They were a matched pair and hung together like two love birds. The difference was Snake Eye had more "go" to him than Moose, but if Moose was behind Snake Eye, he would keep right up. If you put Moose first, then they'd both just poke along. If we had a rider who could ride and wanted to go, we put Snake Eye in the lead; but if we had someone we worried about, we put old Moose in the lead. Old Moose was so fast he could run all day in the shade of a tree and sleep at the roots at night. They were two comical horses.

By the time we got all the horses saddled and the hunters on, Mike had taken another roll of film. I must have packed 100 rolls of film for him, and the way he was going, it might not be enough.

We started up over Randolph Mountain. I told Bill to ride in front of me, and I'd bring the pack horses so Mike could take pictures of Bill in front without anything between Bill and the camera. Mike was having the time of his life. He would trot up in front of us and take a picture, then off to one side and take one; then off to the other side. Then he'd run down the trail behind us and take one. When we got on the other side of Randolph Mountain we were going through a long meadow. Mike was up on the side hill taking pictures when he looked across the canyon and saw the perfect place up the other side to take pictures from. He got on old Snake Eye and kicked him. Off they went down the mountain in a trot. Mike was a big man but a little out of shape. Every time that old horse would trot, Mike would be coming down when Snake Eye went up. They would meet with a big thud and groan. When Mike bounced out of the saddle, you could see a foot of daylight between him and Snake Eye.

Down the side hill they came, trying to run through the pack string. Mike was holding onto the saddle horn with both hands and bouncing a foot off the saddle. They got tangled in the middle of the pack horses. The horses started bucking and fighting, and old Snake Eye slammed on the brakes and stopped on all fours. Mike went right over his head and landed on his back, which knocked the wind out of him. One of the pack horses jumped over the top of him and landed right on his camera. Mike thought he had had it for sure, but when the dust cleared Mike was still alive, although his camera was in four or five pieces.

Mike said he was damn sure thankful it was not him, but this old boy was lost without a camera, so I had to unpack the horse that had the cameras and get him another one. This seemed to make him happy, and off he went across the meadow to get into the spot he had seen to take more pictures. Out in the meadow were some beaver ponds and a lot of willows. Mike and Snake Eye disappeared into the willows, and all of a sudden we could hear Mike holler, "Oh, no," then heard water splashing, and Snake Eye came out of the willows on the run with no Mike.

I got off, tied up the pack horses, and we went to see what was wrong. Mike had tried to ride Snake Eye through one of the beaver ponds. Old Snake Eye sank down into the mud and started lunging to get out and threw Mike off in the middle of the pond. When we got to him he was standing in mud up to his waist and water up to his armpits. He could not work his way out of the mud, but somehow he had his camera above his head in one hand and had kept it from getting ruined. He threw me the camera, then I got a lariat and threw it out to him. We pulled and pulled before we finally got him out of the mud and onto the bank. He looked like a drowned rat!

He tried to talk to me, but he was so cold, his teeth started chattering. So we built a big fire and had him take off his clothes. He looked funny standing there in his birthday suit trying to get warm. I told Slim and Bob that they might just as well take the rest of the hunters and go on into camp. We would be along just as soon as we got Mike warm. I thought that this muddy, wet, predicament would make Mike content just to ride the rest of the way with us, but no, not Mike. As soon as he got on old Snake Eye, away he went, bouncing off the saddle, to get more pictures. He was the most enthusiastic and determined photographer I have ever seen.

We got within a couple of miles of camp, when off the trail, down in a pocket, a moose was standing in a swamp with his head under the water, having lunch. Mike had five or six pictures of him by now, but like most dudes, he wanted a closer one. Old Snake Eye did not like moose. He had had a disagreement with one awhile back on a pack trip in Yellowstone country.

It happened like this: The horses were belled, hobbled, and turned loose.

135

Old Snake Eye and Moose, the horse, had found a meadow above camp that they liked, so they wandered up there. Every morning I would give all the horses grain at camp. That would help keep them from wandering off too far. They all came in for grain that morning except Snake Eye and Moose. I could hear their bells and could tell they were still in the meadow above camp, so I just forgot about them for the day.

The next morning they still did not come in for the grain. I could hear their bells in the meadow, so I decided to go up and bring them down. To get into this meadow, you had to go through a thick patch of timber, and smack-dab in the trail stood this bull moose. There was a swamp on both sides of the trail, and that old bull moose wouldn't let the horses come down. I hollered and threw a stick at him. He slapped the air with his feet and blew out of his nose. I backed off! Old Snake Eye and Moose came out of the timber, and that old moose took a run at them. Snake Eye and Moose, the horse, split up and went on both sides of him. The moose took after Snake Eye, ran him into the swamp, and butted him a couple of times with his horns. Then I really started hollering and throwing rocks. Finally the moose went off into the timber.

Since then Snake Eye would go a mile out of his way to avoid a moose. But Mike, of course, did not know this and kept kicking Snake Eye to get closer to Mr. Moose. They were within ten feet of him when we came around the corner and could see what was happening. By then it was too late to tell Mike—they were right next to the moose. About that time, Mr. Moose jerked his head out of the water and blew water all over Mike and Snake Eye. This scared the moose so bad that he fell down twice trying to get out of the swamp. By this time Snake Eye and Mike were halfway to camp. When the moose blew all over them, Snake Eye went backwards on a run with Mike holding onto the saddle horn with both hands. Seeing Snake Eye run backwards was a hell of a sight. Then he whirled around and up through the timber they went with Mike holding on for dear life and hollering, "Oh shit, help me!"

Snake Eye didn't stop until he got into camp. He ran right up to the cook tent and stood there until Slim came out and got Mike off. Mike and Snake Eye were still shaking when Bill and I got into camp. Mike had dropped his camera during the encounter, but we found it and brought it back to camp. Bill was going to kid Mike and not give it to him until supper time and Mike never mentioned it, not even once.

At supper we were all having a laugh at Mike and his first day's experience getting into camp. Then Bill asked him where his camera was. Mike's face went white and he said, "I must have lost it when the moose was after me." We all laughed and Bill gave it back to him. That put a smile back on Mike's face. Then he put flash bulbs in the camera and took more pictures. Then Mike said his hind end was awfully sore and he was going to bed.

The next morning when I tried to get him up, Mike said he was just too sore to ride, and he was going to stay in camp that day. So Bill and I went hunting without him. The weather was warm and there was lots of grass. This kind of weather makes good camping but tough hunting. We saw one small herd that day but they were out of range.

When we came into camp that evening, Mike was right underfoot as usual taking pictures while we unsaddled, put the saddles away, went into the cook tent, or even went to the outhouse! For two days Mike stayed in camp and took pictures.

We had a woman cook who really liked greasy fried food. Her favorite was pork chops floating in grease and the third day she cooked some for lunch. All the grease gave Mike a stomach ache, and he got the Rocky Mountain Trots! That meant he had to go to the outhouse every five minutes. When we came into camp that night, Mike looked kind of white, and he said he felt really bad. He walked like he had a horse between his legs, but he said he was going hunting the next morning if it killed him!

Bill and I had seen a big bull elk that night just before dark and wanted to get back there before daylight to see if we could catch him out. So we were up and ready to go before daylight. I walked over to Mike where he was already on Snake Eye. I asked him if he had his lunch in the saddle bag and no shell in the barrel of his rifle. He said he was ready to go, but he could use one more roll of film. I went to his tent and brought him one. It was still quite dark as we rode out of camp. Bill was right behind me, and I thought Mike was behind him. We got about a block out of camp and we could hear Mike hollering at the horse. "Get up," then, "Whoa, whoa." In a few minutes, the same thing, and he added, "You damn bull-headed horse," and then he would repeat it all over again. I told Bill we'd better go back and see what was wrong.

When we got back to him, he was still repeating his "Get ups" and "Whoa, whoas", followed by more Scotch blessings. I asked what his problem was, and he said, "This damn horse you gave me is so dumb, he won't leave camp! When I kick him, he starts off and then comes right back." I got off my horse and walked over to take a look. Old Snake Eye was still tied up to the corral! When Mike would kick him, Snake Eye would go until he came to the end of the lead rope, then the lead rope would turn him back to the corral.

When Bill and I found out what had happened, we laughed so hard Bill fell off his horse. Bill said to Mike, "Don't you know the old western saying, 'To get along on a horse, you have to be smarter than the horse you are riding!'" Then Mike laughed and said, "I damn sure haven't felt smarter than a horse the last few days." I untied Snake Eye and we got going. By then it had turned daylight.

By noontime we were in Box Creek. The sun had come out, and it was nice and warm. We found a nice grassy spot where we could see the other side of the canyon, unsaddled the horses, and ate lunch. We sat there for an hour or so talking.

Mike told me about a school teacher, Jane, who worked for him part-time. She took care of the place while he was gone. She did all of the film developing for him and when he got back, she would get all of the pictures of this trip developed first thing. After awhile I suggested saddling up and riding down where we could see some different openings. Mike said, "You guys go right ahead, I'm pretty sore. I'll just wait right here and rest." So we took his horse, but left his saddle and camera and took off.

Bill and I rode down to the bottom of Box Creek and worked our way back up to where Mike was. This took a couple of hours. When we got there, Mike was lying over a dead tree, sound asleep. He had his pants down, with his behind up to the sun! I guess that sun felt mighty good on his sore rear, but that was the worst looking sight I have ever seen. The sores were worse than any saddlesore I have ever seen on a horse.

Bill got off real quietly and got Mike's camera out and proceeded to take a bunch of pictures of poor old Mike. I just couldn't keep from laughing, and we were both laughing so hard, we woke Mike up. He jumped up and hollered, "Oh no," and tried to run behind a tree to hide and get his pants on, but kept tripping on his pants which were still down around his knees. Bill put Mike's camera back into the saddlebags. We laughed so hard we had tears in our eyes. It took quite awhile for Mike to come out from behind that tree. He said he had never been so embarrassed before in his life, but the sun had felt so good on those sores, and that was the first good sleep he had had since coming to camp. I really felt sorry for him. Those sores looked so miserable and bad, yet he had hardly complained. He had to be a tough person. I'll bet he damn sure was a good football player in his day. I know I could not have ridden a horse for two steps in that condition.

We rode slowly back to camp, and I tried to avoid all the rough spots. Bill never told Mike about the pictures we had taken. He said he just didn't have the heart!

138

Two days later the hunt was over. We had to pack up and leave. Mike had not ridden a horse since we took the pictures, but he was still sore as hell. He walked with his legs far apart as if he was on a horse. In fact, I don't think he could tell if he was afoot or horseback! After we got everything packed and ready to go, I asked him if he felt like riding a horse. He said he didn't think he could. I was pretty worried, so I told Slim and Bob to go ahead with the rest of the hunters. Bill and I would poke along with Mike.

Well, needless to say, Mike did not take as many pictures going out as he did coming in, but he did manage to take a few. He would walk a ways, then lie over the saddle like a dead man, and every time the horse stepped, Mike would let out an awful groan.

We got him back to the ranch alive and in one piece that evening. When I took them to the airport and said goodbye, I said, "Be sure and let me know if Mike heals up alright."

About two weeks later I got a phone call from Bill. He told me with laughter in his voice that Mike was almost healed and was in pretty good shape. After they got back, he had Jane develop all the pictures and lay them out on his desk. Mike had not seen them, but he was going to bring a bunch of friends over to look at them. She followed his instructions to the letter along with a note saying "I quit." Of course, there among the pictures were the ones Bill had taken of Mike's backside. He said Mike had not talked to him for a week, but he finally laughed it off.

Later on, Mike sent me some of the pictures he had taken. They sure were very good, but there were none of him, and he never mentioned the backside ones!

The Rancher's Dog

Dan had been a rancher all his life. He was now in his seventies, but was still in good health and took care of his cows by himself. Old Dan was a hard-working and likable kind of man. If a neighbor needed help Dan was right there to give a hand.

A few years ago, in the winter, a car stopped in front of his place and threw a pup out and drove off. That poor pup was not only cold and skinny, but also sick. So Dan's wife made a bed for him behind the stove. They tried to get him to eat, but the pup was too sick and could not eat.

The first three days the dog just lay behind the stove and shook. Dan and his wife had to force-feed him just to keep him alive. The pup looked so bad you could see his backbone and count his ribs. Dan thought for sure the poor little guy was going to die. With their warm, caring, and loving hands, about the fourth day the dog started getting better, and within a week he was as good as new. That dog seemed to sense that they had saved his life. He would follow them everywhere, and, for a pup, you could tell he tried his best to please them.

Dan had two good stock dogs and didn't need another dog. He thought he could find some kid who would want him. After a couple of weeks, he still hadn't found anyone and was growing fond of that pup. He decided to keep him and named him Mike. As time passed, Mike became part of the family. There were times when Dan and Mary would play like they were fighting. Mike would get all excited and bark and growl at Dan. Then he would act like he was going to bite until they would stop. Mike always took Mary's side.

A couple of years later Mary passed away. Dan said, "After Mary was gone, Mike just whined and moped around the house for a couple of weeks." He must have missed Mary almost as much as Dan did. Then, right after that, Dan's daughter, Jane, came to live with him to take care of the house and look after Dan and Mike. By then Dan had really taken a liking to Mike; they were together all the time.

Winter came and the weather turned cold. Dan had a team of horses which he used to feed his cows with in the winter. One morning Dan, Mike, and the other dogs went out to feed. Dan went in the barn and harnessed up the horses and hitched them up to the wagon. He was feeding cows about a mile and a half from the house down in a little draw where the cows had a little wind break.

Dan was on the back of the wagon throwing hay off when he stepped off the wagon and caught his foot in the spokes of the wheel while the team was still moving, Every time the wheel would go around it would twist his leg and flip him over and over, and he could not get his foot out. The pain in his leg was getting unbearable, and he started hollering for help. The hollering spooked the horses, and they started to run. Dan passed out from the pain, and when he came to the wagon had stopped. Then, with all his strength, he managed to get his foot out and crawled away from the wagon. That's when he saw Mike in front of the team of horses with the drive line in his mouth and holding the team there.

Dan hollered to Mike. Mike dropped the lines and ran to Dan. Dan petted him then said, "Mike, old buddy, you've got to go bring help." Mike whined, lay down by Dan's face and licked him then took off for help. When he got to the house the neighbor lady was there visiting Jane. Mike scratched on the front door and barked like hell. Jane came to the door, saw Mike, and thought he had just beaten her father to the house and that he was still out in the barn taking care of the horses. So she told Mike to go back to the barn, then shut the door. Mike whined and barked like hell again and jumped up to the window and barked till Jane came out. Then Mike ran away from the house and stopped and barked at Jane. Jane thought maybe there was something wrong and followed Mike.

There was about five inches of snow on the ground, and it was cold. She found Dan lying by the wagon, passed out and almost frozen to death. Jane ran back to the house and got the pickup and drove it almost to him and got stuck. Then she ran back down to her father and somehow put him on the wagon and drove the team to the house. Lucky thing the neighbor was still there. They both put Dan in her car and took him to the hospital. He had fractured his leg in two places, broken his ankle, and his fingers, toes, and face were frost-bitten. From that day on Dan's nose had a purple color to it from the frost bite. He always said, "I am still alive because of my best friend in the world, Mike."

That accident laid him up for a good year and, in the meantime, he decided to sell all the cows and part of the ranch because it would be a long time before he could take care of them and Jane was working herself to death trying to keep things going. After the accident "Old Dad Time" was starting to show on him. I remember him telling me that, "When you get around my age 'Old Dad Time' has no mercy, but when you are a young man like you, he gives you everything. Then, as the years go by he takes it all back, leaves you bent over, stiff, sore and then takes all your strength away. But I'll have to thank him for one thing—the good friends he gave me." Then he looked at Mike and said, "Especially this one!" All the time he was laid up Mike was with him day and night.

The next winter Dan passed away. The day after his funeral, I got on my horse to bring in the cows off the mountain. I found the cows and started pushing them home. On the way back I had to go by the grave where Dan was buried the day before. There on Dan's grave was Mike. He had Dan's hat under his paw and was whining. I don't think I will ever forget that sight. It choked me up and brought tears to my eyes. I called for Mike and said, "Come on old boy, I will take you home." But he would not leave that grave.

I finished taking the cows home, then I rode over and told Jane where old Mike was. She said she just did not have the heart to take Mike from her father's grave, so my dad went up and got him. After losing Dan, old Mike aged fast. One day, after Jane let him out of the house, he did not come back. After looking for him she found him at Dan's grave. He had passed away. She had him buried next to her mother and father and put on their headstones, "The Best of Friends."

In later years I made a bronze of that dog lying on Dan's grave with his hat. I named it, "I Brought Your Hat, Pard." I wrote a saying that goes with the bronze:

The dog is the only animal that will leave his own for mankind. The dog has been known to be fearless in saving children from drowning and bodily harm and to find them when lost. The dog has given his life protecting humans against overpowering odds, and God only knows how many times he has stopped robbery, accidents, and women from being molested.

Dog . . . ask the blind man how much he is worth. Yet the dog is so gentle I have seen children take him by the ear and lead him around, bite him, practice roping on him, dress him up in old clothes, sit on him, and ride him. Yet the dog will love and protect them with his life.

Loneliness . . . the dog is the ideal companion for older people, children, women, and men.

142

When I was a young boy, after school I would bring the cows off the mountain where I passed the graveyard where an old rancher was buried a few days before. I saw the rancher's dog lying on the grave with his hat.

The sight touched me so, I realized just how faithful and wonderful a dog is.

I have seen a lot of good dogs in my day, but, the two wonderful dogs I will never forget are Mike and my old dog Colie.

Colie, the Dog With a Heart

When I was a young boy, my father did a lot of different things to make a living. There were times when he would buy a load of fruit and vegetables that he would peddle in Vernal and Duchesne country, and a lot of his customers were the Indians who lived there. He had sold and traded a lot of horses in this country in the past few years and had gotten to know some of the Indians quite well.

I remember him telling us boys one day that they were good, down-to-earth kind of people, and all you had to do was treat them square and they would do likewise. He said they talked his language and savvied his brand; that meant they understood each other and had respect for one another. But when it came to horse trading, the Indians and my dad had respect for a shrewd horse trader, and, I'll tell you what, they both were that! I have bought, sold, and traded a few in my days, but I was never in their class, nor have I ever come close.

We took a load of fruit down there and had been peddling it for five days, getting rid of most of the load. All we had left were a dozen bushels of fruit. In the meantime we had picked up: three goats(got rid of two), four horses (sold two and traded two), four sacks of grain, two rifles (traded one), one saddle (sold it), a chicken coop full of chickens (finally sold them), two pigs (still had one), a cowboy hat (did not fit), a box of tools, and a truckload of cedar posts (sold them). My dad said that he knew a friend by the name of Running Elk who needed a goat and pig, and we needed to take shed of those two animals, so we went to see him.

He lived down in the bottom of a canyon. The road in there was rougher than hell and cut along the side of a cliff. When we got into the bottom it opened up into a beautiful valley and had lots of good grass and a good stream of water. On the other side of the creek was Running Elk's cabin nestled in a bunch of cottonwoods. He had good corrals and a barn. The

144

stream had no bridge, and the water was up to the running boards when we drove through it. As we drove up to the cabin, here came four dogs and a litter of pups. Two of the dogs looked like they were border collies and the other two Australian shepherd mix. Out of the cabin came Running Elk, his wife, and boy. They knew my dad and were glad to see him.

Running Elk stood a little higher than the average man and was slim-built. He had a dark face and wrinkles from being out in the sun, but he was a good-looking man. His wife was slim and beautiful. She had long, black hair, a pretty face with a pleasant, bright smile. Their boy was a stout looking kid. He was a few years older than me. They greeted us with such warmth and friendship that Dad just gave them the goat. They insisted we have lunch with them. We had elk and antelope steaks, fresh, sweet carrots; tomatoes; peas and corn from the garden; and some cold, sweet goat milk. So we all sat down, pitched in and shoveled till we won. I'll tell you, that was one fine meal.

After supper we went out to the corrals to see their new colts. One of those little pups followed me down to the corrals and stayed right on my heels all the time. He was so cute that I just had to play with him. As I remember, the colts were a colorful bunch. It looked like the colors must have rubbed off a rainbow; pintos, palominos, steel grey, and a sorrel with a flax mane and tail. Running Elk had a good-looking pinto stud which he said he was out of his best range mare and out of a running quarter horse stud. My dad tried to talk him out of that horse, but Running Elk said he wasn't hurting to trade, and he was pretty well-mounted. Anyway, he had given him to his boy, and he was no "Indian trader!" They all laughed.

Back at the cabin Running Elk and Dad went to trading. As I remember, Running Elk ended up with the pig, three sacks of grain, the cowboy hat, (that did not fit him either), and six bushels of fruit. My dad got some money and a 25-35 rifle with a hexagon barrel. Then Running Elk threw in the black female pup that kept following me. He told us the pup's mother was one of his border collies but the father had been a stray—a 79-Heinz. Dad told Running Elk that by the time he was through trading with him, he couldn't tell if he was afoot or horseback! Both laughed and shook hands, then we said goodbye and left. I can't remember meeting any warmer or nicer people than they were.

From there we went to town and stopped in front of the pool hall. There were a few old Indians sitting outside and my dad knew some of them. He sold the rest of the fruit. This one Indian wanted the pup so my dad traded her to him. I cried and put up such a fuss that after we had left and gone a mile, he decided he had better go back and get that pup.

Well, this Indian was a horse trader, and when my Dad told him he had to have the pup back, the Indian sensed the want. He had given my dad a horse bridle and a pair of spurs for the pup, which was a lot for a mutt pup. Dad had to give $8.00 and the bridle and spurs to get her back. He said, "I don't know why you want that pup. She is just a mutt and that's more than a pup is worth." Dad was mad, and he made me keep her in the back all the way home and wouldn't have a thing to do with her.

My dad had an old dog he thought the world of. When he got on his horse the dog was ready to go. He always went with him, and when the dog got tired Dad would say, "Come on up." That dog would jump up behind the saddle and lay sideways till my Dad stopped or told him to get off. He never let anyone, including us kids, pet or play with him. He said that pampering a dog would ruin him, and he wouldn't let him in the house. But that dog was sure a good stock dog, and he always went with us when we had stock to work.

We named the little black pup Colie, and as she got older, you could see she had a little collie in her. You could tell by the way she acted around cows that she had cow sense. We had had her for about five months when one day we could not find our steers. Dad was out in the desert trapping wild horses, and us kids had been looking for those steers for five days without finding them.

When my dad got home from running horses he saddled his old saddle horse and went looking for the steers, taking his old dog, and he let Colie follow. After for or five hours of looking he picked up their trail and tracked them till dark without finding them. He turned around and rode home in the dark. His old dog got tired, so he let him up behind the saddle, but he could not find Colie. He figured that she had played out on him, lay down in the brush some place, and would come home the next day. He got home about midnight, put his horse in the corral, fed and grained him, and went to bed.

The next morning he was getting ready to go looking for the steers when, low and behold, there in the corral stood the steers, and Colie was sitting in the middle of the gate holding them in. About the time it takes to snap your fingers my dad fell in love with that dog, and it was not long after that he was bragging to everyone about that little dog and how he had got her for practically nothing! I'll tell you what, you couldn't have bought her then for a thousand dollars. Colie must have sensed that Dad was after those steers after tracking them all day, and when dark came and Dad turned back, she must have tracked them into the night till she found

146

them and drove them home. Then she sat in the middle of the gate till my dad came out the next morning.

You can train a dog all its life and not teach it what Colie picked up by herself with not much training at all. It seemed that if you could just give her an idea she would learn the rest. Everyone in the family loved her. One by one, they all put their brand on her, but I still thought she belonged to me.

My parents had never let a dog in the house before, but my mother liked that dog so well she'd let her in the house and made sure she got the best of food. Dad would act like he was throwing a fit when Mother let her in the house. He said that between Mother and us kids we were pampering her too much, and she would loose her cow sense. But I remember seeing him let her in at night and, at times, lying on the foor playing with her.

Colie had never attempted to bite nor had she even growled at anyone before, until one day when a bill collector came to the door. As usual, we were damn short on money. My mother was telling him she wanted to pay him half now and the rest next month. He was mad and hollering at her in a loud voice. He said he wanted it all and right now. Colie started to growl. The bill collector said, "Shut that mutt up!" and reached out and jerked the money out of my mother's hand. That was a big mistake! Colie jumped up, the bill collector slammed the screen door for protection, but Colie jumped right through the screen and grabbed him by the arm and bit him. He took off running, but Colie ripped both pantlegs off him before he could get to his car.

Two months later the bill collector took my dad to court. To make a long story short, the judge asked Dad what had happened. Dad told the judge how the bill collector had hollered at my mother and grabbed the money out of her hand. The bill collector's lawyer said that didn't make any difference. "Just what, Mr. Lemmon, are you going to do about it?" My dad answered, "I'll tell you waht I'm going to do, I'm going to buy that dog the biggest steak in Juab County." The judge banged his desk with his hammer and said, "Case dismissed!" That was before lawyers made a million out of a court case.

My mother's family were sheep people and my dad used to take them supplies. One day, Dad said to me, "Would you like to go with me to take supplies out to your uncle?" He didn't have to ask twice. Colie and I jumped in the truck and away we went. My uncle was running his sheep on Maple Mountain, and it took us half a day of driving on dusty dirt roads to get there. We got there toward evening and my uncle was just coming out of his sheep wagon to bring the sheep in for the night. He invited us to go along.

He saddled another horse for Dad, and I rode bareback. My uncle had four of the best sheep dogs in the country, and he took two of them along. We found the sheep on the other side of the canyon. My uncle hollered at his dogs, then pointed at the sheep and said, "Fetch them home." His dogs took off down in the canyon with Colie right behind them. If my uncle could see the sheep, then all he had to do was point and holler and his dogs would fetch the sheep to camp.

To a sheep man, a dog that could do this was worth their weight in gold, and it took an extra-smart dog to learn. To train one took months and sometimes a year or better. Some dogs never could learn. We stayed and helped my uncle for three days.

On the morning of the third day we helped him move camp. Every day, at least once and sometimes twice, my uncle would have the dogs bring the sheep in close to camp just by pointing in their direction and hollering. Colie went with the dogs each time and seemed to enjoy doing it. After moving camp that morning we were getting ready to leave. My dad and uncle were having a drink and Dad got to bragging about Colie. My uncle told him he thought Colie was an awfully smart dog, but it would take her a few months running with the sheep before she could learn to bring them to camp. My dad said she could do it right now. I knew he would not have said that if he had not been drinking, but they bet five dollars on it.

From where we were you could see the sheep grazing on a hillside about three miles off. My uncle tied his dogs up. Dad walked out in the open, hollered at Colie, and pointed at the sheep. She whined for a few seconds then ran down the hill, turned around, and came back. Dad took her head, held it in the direction of the sheep and said, "Go fetch", and away she went. We couldn't see her for fifteen or twenty minutes, then she came out of the brush just below the sheep. My uncle turned to me and said, "I don't believe it! No dog can learn that quick!"

I don't think Dad was ever so proud of a dog in his life. I know I was proud, and she put a tear in my eye. My uncle wanted to trade his four dogs just for Colie, but he knew he could have offered his camp and all his sheep and it wouldn't have done any good. Colie, after all, was part of the family.

In the late spring all of the herders in the country drive their sheep to the train station on a certain date to have them shipped to the summer range. This station sat out in the desert and the name of it was Jericho. The railroad would have help there to load the sheep, and the loading

148

would last for about a week depending on how many sheep there were to ship. The herders would scatter out from the station for a few miles holding their sheep together and waiting for their turn to load.

My uncle was there, and he still had a good day to wait. Dad and I were there visiting him. I got restless, so I took my dog and went up to the loading corrals to watch them load the sheep. In the loading pens there was a big, red-headed man loading sheep. He had a goat and a couple of dogs to help. If you have never seen a goat load sheep it is something to see. The goat will walk around the corrals getting the sheep to follow him, then he'll go up the loading ramp into the boxcar with the sheep following him, circle the car and come back out. By the time I got there the goat and one dog were played out. The red-head was on his last dog, and that dog was tired so it wasn't long until he quit him, too. The man was so mad he started throwing sheep up the ramp and cussing up a storm. He looked at me and Colie, walked over and asked me if that dog could work sheep. I said, "Yes." He said he had two more cars to load before the day was over, and he would pay me to use that dog. I had to ponder on it a spell, then said, "If she gets tired I'll have her stop and take her home." He said that was fine. I got in the corrals and got her to working the sheep. It took but a short time and we had the boxcars loaded. He gave me the money, grabbed Colie and said, "I'll give you twenty dollars for this dog." I said, "She is not for sale. I want you to give her back to me." He said, "I'll keep this dog until tomorrow." I started crying and grabbed my dog and he pushed me down. That was a big mistake! Colie grabbed his arm and drew blood and he dropped her. She chewed on both of his legs and he was yelling, "Help me, stop this dog, please!"

I grabbed hold of Colie and over the fence we went, running all the way back to my uncle's camp. Dad asked me what was wrong and I told him. He went down to the loading station, mad as hell, kicking up dust like a Brahma bull. By the time he got there the red-head had gone to town to see a doctor. My dad told the man who ran the place that when the red-head came back he was going to stomp the hell out of him. The boss said he had had a lot of trouble with him, and he would not be coming back.

Some of the things Colie had learned to do were unbelievable, like playing hide and seek. From playing that game with us kids she had learned to lie down, put her paws over her eyes and stay in that position for a couple of minutes, then jump up and come running to look for us . . . and she always found us. She had learned to ride on the back of a horse just like my Dad's old dog and had learned that in two short lessons. One

149

thing she loved to do was go swimming with us. We would call her up on the diving board, and she would jump off.

As I remember, it was in the fall and the whole family was out hunting. To my family hunting season was our big holiday. Dad always said that if we were rich instead of so damn poor and had a chance to go to Hawaii or around the world, we would still rather load up the old ponies, get all the family together, and go hunting. Getting game was not so important as was the going. Although, if it were not for deer, elk, and antelope, we would have starved to death!

We had been out hunting for four days when here came the sheriff all excited. A family from California was hunting over on the other mountain, and their little girl was lost. She had been missing for two days now. The nights were getting colder. They had a search party out but had not found her yet. They were bringing in some hound dogs, but they would not get there until tomorrow. Then the sheriff remembered Colie. He had seen and heard of some of the things she had done and thought she could help find the little girl. Dad didn't wait to answer. He called Colie, and they all jumped in the sheriff's car and took off in a cloud of dust to look for her.

When they got to where the little girl's family had been camping, the girl's mother and father were in hysterics. The first thing Dad did was get a piece of the little girl's clothes for Colie to get her scent. It was impossible to track her because there were too many horse and people tracks from all the people looking for her.

He took the sheriff's horse, got some water and food and told Colie to get up on the horse with him. The sheriff and some of the boys wanted to go but my dad said no, because if he did pick up her tracks, then all the people and horses would just make more tracks and cause more confusion. But with just him, she could concentrate and find the little girl better. He rode out about five miles then got off his horse. He had Colie smell the girl's clothes then started to circle the camp. After about five hours Colie picked up her tracks. By then it was getting later and colder.

They tracked her till dark but had not found her. Dad sat down to think it over and take a rest, but Colie would have nothing to do with that. She ran off barking at Dad, then came back, whined, then took off again. Dad knew Colie could track at night. She had proven that when she brought the steers in after dark. He got on his horse and said to Colie, "Let's go find the little girl." Dad had to trot his horse to keep up with Colie. Something inside of that dog must have told her that they did not have much time left. Where that little dog got her sense from, only God knows.

150

They finally found the little girl about midnight lying under a cedar tree and almost gone from exhaustion, hunger, and exposure. Her whole body was ice-cold. Dad put his coat around her, and Colie laid down beside her and cuddled up close. Dad built a big fire, then gave her some food and water. The little girl fell for Colie. She put both arms around her and would not turn loose all night. Colie didn't seem to mind. I think she fell for the little girl, too.

About daylight Dad put her in the saddle, got behind her, and started home. After a little ways he could tell she was getting frightened, and he told Colie to jump up in the saddle with her. The little girl put her arms around Colie and that seemed to make her feel better. They took her to the hospital, but she kept crying for Colie. Dad said, "Let the dog stay with her, and I'll come back and get her later."

The word of Colie saving the little girl spread through the county. She was a hero, and, I'll tell you what, she damn-well deserved it. Through the years she had three litters of pups. We gave some of them to my uncle, and he trained them for sheep dogs. They all made good ones, but none was like Colie. Mother and Dad gave some to special friends and sent one female pup that looked just like Colie to the little lost girl in California. They send back two hundred dollars and a lot of pictures of the pup and the little girl playing with her. They named the pup Colie! Mother sent the money back but kept the pictures. She put the one of the girl playing with little Colie above the fireplace where she could look at it.

We had a list a mile long of people who wanted to buy her next pups. Dad said she could have one more litter then he would take her to the

vet to get fixed. A few months later she came in heat. Dad gave us strict orders to watch and don't let any dog get next to her.

Part of the way my Father made a living was running wild horses and using them to put on rodeos. He and my older brothers had corraled a bunch and were out in the desert bringing them in.

On this particular day my Mother was at our aunt's house visiting for the day. My brother and I were out in the yard playing with Colie, when one of the neighbors came by and was going to town. He wanted to know if we would like to go. We put Colie in the shed and tied her up, then shut the door so that no dogs could get to her while we were gone. The shed had a window about five feet off the floor and had no glass in it. While we were gone Colie jumped out the window. The rope was long enough to let her jump out, but too short to let her reach the ground, and she hung herself to death.

Before we got home my mother got there and went in the house to get supper ready. When we got back the neighbor let us out in front of the house. We said our thanks and started for the house. The shed was out in back of the house and the window was in the back part of the shed; you couldn't see the window from the house. On our way in, I hollered for Colie. She didn't answer. I thought she was in the house with my mother.

After we got in the house, mother asked where Colie was. My brother said, "If she's not in the house, she still must be locked in the shed." Mother said, "You two go get her out of that shed right now!" We went out to the shed and found her hanging there. The sight was like getting electrocuted, the shock just numbed us both, then we both started crying.

My Mother saw me from the window and came out to the shed. She saw Colie hanging there. I will never forget the sight of my mother on her knees with both arms wrapped around Colie and crying.

I know that when a living soul reaches the end of their trail and goes over that Great Divide, the good Lord has a special place for them, and especially for a dog like Colie. There was not a person in our family who did not cry from the heartbreak and the loss of that little old dog. She was part collie and the other part mutt, but that goes to show that people, horses, and dogs don't have to be thoroughbreds to be the very best!

The word of her dying spread because people came from miles around just to say how bad they felt, Dad would be out on the desert for a few more days wrangling the horses, and we had no way to tell him. We buried her on a hill in back of the house, under an old cedar tree. That was the place she had liked best.

152

Sheep Hunting

To most hunters, the thought of going hunting, to be out in the mountains with a good horse under them, and having a chance of getting a big trophy chills the blood and gives them the excitement that a kid gets on Christmas morning. Well, Pardner, there's one kind of hunt that has that special kind of feeling to it—sheep hunting.

It is done mostly above timberline where you are a long way from church but a lot closer to God. Just sit back on your old pony, relax, take time to look around, and you feel it—the air is so clean. Spring pops out of the ground, and the water is clear, sweet, and ice-cold. Those beautiful, lush green meadows run for miles, with those dainty, sparkling mountain flowers in all colors of the rainbow. The clouds look like you can almost touch them, and you can see for miles in all directions. The sight and feeling of it all takes your breath away.

That's why I was so excited one morning when I got a phone call from Joe in New Mexico. He had a sheep permit for Area 10 and wanted me to take him hunting. He had gotten my name from his neighbor whom I had taken elk hunting a few years before. We made the arrangements and he booked for the first of September. He asked if he could bring a friend, Howard, along for company. Howard had never been hunting before and was not much of a hand with a horse, but was a good cook and liked helping around camp.

Between the time that Joe called and the first of September, Howard called me four or five times to ask different questions and find out if he could bring along some of his own special recipes and the gatherings to cook them.

It was the end of August and I was just getting ready to pack in our base camp where we would be hunting from. Joe and Howard had asked if they could come a few days early, help set up camp, and stay so they could look the country over and get a little used to riding the horses. This sounded good to me because then I wouldn't have to make an extra trip out just to get them.

We had a cook quit the week before the hunt, so old Slim volunteered, after a little coaxing, to come along and do the cooking, take care of the horses, and look after camp for us. Slim said when he was younger he cooked lots of beans for fifteen or twenty cowhands for a cow outfit in Montana on roundups. He let us know right off that the first one to complain was going to do the cooking for the rest of the trip!

After we got that all settled, we packed the horses, strung them out, and up the trail we went. About five hours later we turned off the trail and headed up a canyon that had no horse trail, just an old game trail to follow. We fought the brush and timber until we finally reached a nice patch of timber at timberline. There was a little spring and lots of grass for the horses, so we set up camp.

While I unpacked and took care of the horses, Slim cooked up a big pot of beans, some sourdough bread, and coffee. It was pretty good grub. Having known Slim all these years I couldn't help but wonder how his cooking was going to be. His beans and sourdough went down pretty good, but he sure made stout coffee!

The next morning when we got up, Slim had breakfast on the table— beans, sourdough bread, and coffee! He said, "Grub is on boys, sit down, pitch in, and shovel 'til you win." Now beans are not my specialty for breakfast, and by the looks on Joe's and Howard's faces they felt the same way, but we managed to get it down. While we ate, Slim fixed our lunch and packed our saddlebags. Then Joe, Howard, and I got on the horses and left camp. We wanted to look the country over and see if we could find out where the sheep were hanging out.

By noon we had worked our way up to a high out-cropping of rocks. With our spotting scopes, we located some sheep on the other side of the canyon. There were twelve head of them feeding at the edge of a patch of timber, but there was not a legal ram in the bunch.

Howard said, "I'm getting hungry," so he got our lunch out—sourdough bread, a can of pork and beans, and a little bag of coffee. Three meals of beans in a row made them hard to look at, let alone eat. Besides we were getting a little gas, but we were hungry and had nothing else, so we got them down.

By the end of the day we had spotted quite a few sheep but no legal rams. The next morning was the first of September, the opening of sheep season, so we went back to camp for a good night's sleep.

When we got there Slim came out of the tent and said, "Supper is on the table, pitch in, and I'll take care of the horses." We walked in the tent and there on the table for supper were—beans, coffee, sourdough, and for a little change, some peaches. We ate the bread and peaches, but none of us touched the beans.

When Slim came in I said, "Good hell, man, those beans are getting hard to eat." Then I remembered what he said before we left about the first one who complained, so I stopped before I went any further. He was looking at me out of the corner of his face, his eyes squinted, and a big smile on his whiskered mug. So to smooth things over I went on to say, "They might be terrible to eat, but they are sure good." Joe looked at Slim and said, "I'm getting a stomach ache from eating them." Slim smiled at him and said, "Ho, ho." Joe came right back with, "I guess the reason I'm getting a stomach ache is because they are so good I can't stop eating them!" Slim asked Howard what he thought. Howard went for it like a dry steer that just smelled fresh water and said, "Slim, I think you are a good cook when it comes to beans and sourdough, but I brought the makings for one of my special French breakfasts, and I would like to give you a break in the morning and cook it up." This caused old Slim to smile and seemed to make the rest of his day.

Old Slim was a man that Mother Nature did not lay a kindly hand on. He was born of poorly looks and was so bow-legged you could run a steer between his legs without knocking him over. He was so skinny he had to stand twice to make a shadow. His two front teeth were missing and really showed when he smiled. He never said an unkind word about his fellow man or abused dumb animals. He was just glad to be alive and have any kind of a chance at life's game. I can damn sure tell you what this breed of man would do for a friend when the chips were down and the trail got rough.

The next morning, Howard was up early getting breakfast and sounding like he was having a good time doing it, singing like an old lonesome coyote. He cooked up a mighty good meal—eggs with a lot of cheese, potatoes with cream and cheese, rice with cream and cheese, but the rice wasn't done. Howard didn't know that in this high altitude it took longer to cook everything. It was hard as pea gravel, but the rest of the breakfast was real good chewing. He had been a chef for a fancy restaurant back East, but had never cooked out in the brush before nor over an open fire. I'll tell you his cooking was a relief from old Slim's beans.

After breakfast we rode out of camp just after daylight. We worked our way up to a high basin where we had spotted some sheep the day before.

A lot of sheep hunting is sitting in one spot for hours, using field glasses, and scoping the mountain sides for sheep. There have been times I have covered the side of the hill with my glasses and not seen a thing, then just as I was going to leave, taken one more look and spotted a ram that had been lying down and gotten up to feed. After we had scoped this area for a couple hours with no luck, we decided to climb up to the opposite side of the mountain. It was too steep and cliffy for horses so we had to leave them.

There are tricks to every trade. Above timberline where there are no trees to tie the horses to and you have two or more horses, you turn them in opposite directions and tie their lead ropes to each other's saddle horn. Then all they can do is go around in circles, but make sure that there are no steep dropoffs or cliffs close by, because they could work their way to them and go over the side. I have had to leave horses tied up this way three to four hours at a time, and they have always been there when I came back and had not moved much. Well, we tied our horses this way, climbed to some cliffs, and crossed over to the other side. By then my belly button was rubbing blisters on my backbone, and my stomach must have thought my throat was cut, I was so hungry.

We sat in a nice grassy spot on the hillside where we could see a lot of country, opened our lunch, and guess what? We had sourdough, the last of Slim's beans, and Howard's uncooked rice! Joe took one look at lunch, and his face turned four different shades of color. He looked like he had been thunderstruck and said, "Oh shit, I'd rather eat buffalo chips." I had to laugh, and right there in front of me were some sheep droppings, so I picked up a handful and said, "How about some sheep raisins for dessert?" He looked at them, laid on his back and laughed like hell. I said, "Root, hog or die, I'm starved, so I'm going to eat them beans and rice." You know, we were so hungry that they went down real easy. Later, Joe said that if he ate that stuff at home, he'd develop an ulcer, but up here hunting, you work your body so hard that you can eat just about anything and your system will digest it, except maybe buffalo chips.

We sat there scoping for a couple of hours and finally spotted four nice legal rams. They were way across the canyon and lying in the middle of a little basin. There was no way we could get over there before dark. To get there we would have to climb down to the bottom of the big canyon, then scratch our way up through a series of cliffs to get within shooting distance of them. We watched them until almost dark and tried to figure out how to get over there and from what directions to approach them. It looked like it was around 500 to 600 yards from where they were lying

156

to the nearest cover. We decided that the only way to get up early in the morning, take our packs with sleeping bags and grub, then work our way over there, and maybe from there we could figure out how to approach them.

Back at camp that night Slim said he would ride up with us as far as we could get the horses, then bring them back to camp, because we would have to stay out at least overnight and maybe a couple of nights. Howard said he'd like to come along. I said that would be all right but warned him there would be a lot of hiking, and we would have to rough it a little and live off what we could carry on our backs. He said that sounded good to him, and he'd even do the cooking. I told him to get some grub ready and be sure to bring some dehydrated food so that we wouldn't be carrying a lot of extra weight.

The next morning we were up and in the saddle right after daylight and made good time riding up to where we had to leave the horses. Slim left with the horses, and we put our packs on our backs and started climbing down the mountain to the bottom of the canyon.

By noon we were on the other side climbing through some cliffs. The wind was starting to blow pretty hard, so we found a little spring and some cover and decided to hole up there until the weather calmed down. We got in behind a couple of rocks, and Howard started laying our grub out on a big flat rock.

By now the wind was kicking up dust and sand. Howard got out the butter, pulled the paper off, cut a slice off, looked at it, then shook his head and threw it away. He cut another slice, shook his head and threw it away. He did it again and again until there was no butter left. I couldn't figure out just what the hell he was doing, so I went over to him and asked him why he sliced up the butter and threw it away. He said, "Vic, when I get back home and tell this story, no one will believe me, but the wind blew so hard that it blew sand clear through the butter." I had to laugh and tried to explain to him that the wind could not really blow sand through the butter. Instead, every time he sliced a piece off, the wind would blow fresh sand on the clean slice. He still thought the wind blew the sand clear through, and he still believes it to this day, no matter how hard I tried to explain otherwise.

The wind kicked up a storm, it started raining, then turned to snow, so we decided to spend the night there. When we got up the next morning it had cleared off, and within a couple hours the snow was almost gone. We had a little breakfast and started hiking up the side of the hill. In a couple of hours we came to the spot where we could see into the basin where the sheep had been two days ago. They weren't there! I did not want to get too much closer and take the chance of spooking them out of the country if they were still around, but after looking for them half the morning and still not finding them, we decided to work our way up a little higher.

Off to our left and up the hill there was a high outcropping where it looked like we could see into the basin at a different angle, so we slipped down the hill a little and worked our way back up to the high spot. By now it was getting towards afternoon. We settled down on the high spot, took shed of our packs, got out the field glasses, and within a few minutes we found the rams. They were lying down behind some rocks, almost in the same place we had first spotted them. After awhile, one of them got up and started to feed, but from where we were it was an awfully long shot.

We decided the best way to stalk them was for Howard to stay there while Joe and I went a little higher and got on the other side of the ridge, going until we got beyond the sheep so we would be downwind of them. We would then come back over on this side of the mountain and slip down behind a pile of rocks that was in the direction the sheep were feeding. When we got there, Howard was to give us hand signals and let us know where the sheep were.

© gary sheep

158

We started working our way over. It was so steep that in places we had to get on our hands and knees just to keep our balance because the whole side of the hill was loose gravel. We finally got to where I figured we were below the sheep. We crossed back over the ridge to the side the sheep were on, and I had guessed it just right. We came out right behind the big rocks, using them for cover, and then we slipped down to the bottom of the basin, working our way slowly and carefully, until we got to the point where we figured the sheep were feeding. We could see the bottom, top, and some of the middle of the basin, but no sheep. We could see Howard, and he gave us hand signals that let us know that the sheep were heading in our direction.

It was getting late, but all we could do was wait and hope they would feed where we could see them before dark. The sun went down, and within just a few minutes a small ram came into the open where we could see him. We studied him with the field glasses. He was barely legal, but Joe decided he didn't want him because he was too small. It was getting close to being too dark to shoot when out came another ram, this one a good legal ram. Joe laid over a rock and shot, killing him instantly. He was a nice ram—heavy horns with a tight curl. We dressed him out by flashlight, then put him on our backs and found our way back to where Howard was waiting for us.

It was a couple hours after dark by then, so we rolled out our sleeping bags and spent the night on the side of the mountain. The next morning we got up, had breakfast, and carried the sheep out to where we could pick him up with the horses, then went to camp.

When you are sheep hunting there are times when you can set up camp at the edge of timberline in a nice patch where there is wood and water. The timber gives you protection from the wind, rain, and sun that you can't find above timberline. Quite often to get into sheep country, you have to take shed of the comforts of camp and horses, put a pack on your back with your grub and bedroll and hike into some mighty rough country. Sometimes you have to scratch your way to the top of mountains or cliffs and spend a few days out with whatever you carried on your back. It is strenuous and damned hard work at times, but Pardner, there is a clean, unchanged freedom that makes it all worthwhile—like the Indians and mountain men must have felt before man plowed the buffalo grass upside down and planted his asphalt.

The Guide

few years ago I hired a guide by the name of Tom. He was part Indian and lived near Lander, Wyoming. The first time I met him he was hauling horses for an outfit that rented horses to dude ranches and hunting camps. He said his job ended the end of October. That fit right in because, that is when I needed a guide for a couple of hunts. In the meantime he got hurt. We was down in the back of a stock truck unloading horses when a horse kicked him and broke his leg.

It was the end of October when Slim and I had just finished a ten day hunt and had brought the hunters back to the ranch. The next hunt started the next day, and that was when I needed Tom. That night he came to the ranch in his old truck with his saddle horse, bedroll, and a damned broken leg with a cast that went from his hip clear down to his foot with only his toes sticking out!

I took one look at him and said, "My hell, man, what have you been tangling with? A jealous husband or what?" I told him that he would not have to guide, that I would get someone else.

He said, "Buffalo chips," and a few other things. "I can guide with a broken leg better than most can with two good legs." I scratched my head and thought, well, we have a wrangler in camp who can help him, if he has to; besides, with such short notice I didn't think I could find someone else to replace him. The hunting had been getting better. The deep snow had been pushing the elk out of Yellowstone, so there was a good chance that a couple of hunters would fill up in a few days, then we could relieve old Tom and let him stay in camp.

I had a friend in town who had been helping me all summer with pack trips. He was Bob Bovie, a music teacher. This old boy could play any musical instrument and make an organ sound like a hummingbird. He was not the best hand with a horse, but damn good around camp. Bob

160

came from Ohio and had a good education. Bob was going to hunting camp with us to help around camp and hunt a little.

The next morning we packed up the horses, and old Tom was right in the middle doing his share and dragging that cast around in the snow. His track looked like someone had dragged a log behind a horse. I told him to sit down, that we would take care of the packing. I was finding out that Tom felt like he had to do his share.

He said, "I can handle my end," and went right on packing and telling jokes. Things went fine, and we got into camp a couple of hours before dark. The cook went right into the cook tent and started getting the grub on. We unsaddled the pack horses, and the wrangler rounded up the saddle horses for the morning hunt and put them in the corral. We belled and hobbled the rest of the horses and gave them a good feeding of grain. By now, old Tom's tracks were all over camp. It looked like someone was plowing snow. We had a big tent put up for all the guides to sleep in. After supper that night, we all talked around the table awhile and told some stories, but mostly we listened to Tom. He never seemed to run out; he was the kind of person you liked right off.

Before going to bed that night, I tried to draw him a map of the country so he would have an idea where to go in the morning. He said, "I will make out, I don't need a map." We all got into bed except Bob and Tom. They stayed up and kept talking and arguing.

Bob had been out with me on pack trips that summer, and every night after everyone had bedded down, Bob would stay up and keep the fires going. He never slept much, four to five hours a night, and the bedroll he slept in didn't weigh more than three to four pounds. It couldn't keep a polar bear warm, and when he did decide to bed down he could lie anywhere, including on a sharp rock, and sleep like a baby! One difference between Tom and Bob was, Tom always had a shot of "red eye" on him!

Tom's two hunters were from Chesapeake Bay. One was a doctor and the other a bookkeeper named Dennis. Slim's two hunters were from Phoenix, Arizona, and were brothers. One of mine was from California and the other from Texas.

The next morning we were in the saddle before daylight. I started riding off towards Gravel Mountain, and Tom and his two hunters were right behind us. Just as we started into the first meadow Tom turned and went up the mountain into some black timber that was full of downfall.

I hollered at him, told him it was a jungle up there and no trail. He answered back, "I know!" and away he went. I thought to myself those boys from Chesapeake Bay are in for a hard day! In the cook tent last night they both told me they had not seen such high mountains and big country in their lives. This was their first hunt, except for birds and squirrels.

We started to see quite a few signs, which looked like a lot of elk on the move. The snow was about eight inches deep. We were working our way up Gravel Mountain when we ran into a herd of elk. There were two spikes in the herd; both hunters got in some shooting and got one. We cleaned and quartered him, then headed back to camp. It had been awhile since I had been in camp this early in the day. My last hunters liked staying out all day.

The two hunters went into their tents and took a nap, so I went on out to look at the horses when I heard someone coming up the trail cussing like hell. I looked up and there was old "Preacher." We called him Preacher because he claimed to have been one at one time. He had a pack string of mules and was packing for an outfit that had a couple of camps. One was by Enos Lake and the other up by Two Ocean Pass.

A few years before, a couple of mules had wandered into our camp with their packs on, and that is when I first met Preacher. I caught them and put them in the corral and a few hours later here came Preacher cussing up a storm! They had gotten loose and disappeared like smoke in the woods. I told him to tie up those long-eared critters and come on in and have a cup of coffee to warm his belly. We had a hot drink that was very good on cold days. We called it a Camp Special—1 cup hot water, 4 tablespoons Tang, 2 teaspoons of honey, and (depending on how cold it was) a splash or two of brandy. Some day when it's cold try one!

Preacher was not too big a guy. He had gray hair and whiskers and a smiling face that looked like Santa Claus. He had packed and guided for many years, and every year he would say, "This is my last time, this life is too hard on an old man." But every year he would come back. We always looked foward to having him stop and visit.

We talked awhile and then went into the cook tent to have a Camp Special. He told me that the camp he was packing for was getting elk. It had snowed a foot and a half in Yellowstone and the elk seemed to be heading for the feed ground.

Old Preacher walked with a limp. He said that a mule had kicked him in the hip a few years ago and cracked it. He was alone at the time and ten miles from camp, and he had to ride the mule that kicked him. He couldn't sit up straight so he laid over the saddle like a dead man in order to ride out of there, then drove to Jackson to the hospital. His hip had bothered him ever since. He had a big scar on his shoulder from when a mule he was breaking to pack bit him. But he still loved mules!

162

He once told me that years ago, when he had around forty head of mules, he would ride one and trail the rest to New Mexico for the winter. He would do odd jobs like skidding firewood and timber. The winters down there are a lot milder and shorter, and he could work them most of the winter. Then, come spring, he would trail them back to Wyoming and use them for packing for the Forest Service and different outfits through the summer.

As for the mules he had now, he called one Pretty Girl (ha, ha, ha), and one Pretty Boy (another ha, ha, ha), and then there were Zeke, Zeb, Pardner, Brown Eyes, Prairie Rose, Sweetheart, Clementine, and Side Kick. They were big mules and had a hell of a walk to them. A good looking bunch as far as mules go.

The cook fixed up some grub, and then Preacher got his mules strung out and up the trail he went. The one he called Clementine was always put at the end of the string and every time he would start off she would bray like a coyote and wring her tail. This time she started braying, and off in the timber, an old bull elk answered. We damn sure got a belly laugh out of that!

Just at dark Tom and his two hunters came in. His hunters looked mighty tired. Doc had busted the stock on his rifle. Earlier that day his horse had slipped on ice and went into a tree, so Tom lent him his rifle. They rode to Pacific Creek and back, which was a hell of a long ride. His hunters only ate a sandwich and went right to bed. But not Tom, he still had half the night to go. His cast was starting to come apart from getting wet. I asked him if he would like to put a plastic bag around it to keep it from getting worse but he said it was all right and began telling stories.

He told Bob a hunting story of when he was hunting in the Wind River country with his 30-06 and came upon a bull elk standing on a side hill. He shot him through the heart, and come to find out, there was another five-point standing along side of him and the shell had gone through his heart, too. Then it ricocheted off a rock and killed a pine hen sitting in a tree, veered up into the sky and hit a crow that was flying by. Well, old Bob, the school teacher, was hellacious on rifle ballistics, and he told Tom a 30-06 couldn't do all that. Tom answered, "That's not all, after it went so high it lost its power, it came back down just as a big black bear was passing by and killed him, too." Bob just shook his head and gave up.

Later that night, in the guide tent, we all went to sleep except Bob and Tom. They stayed awake talking and arguing. A good thing about having those two in your camp is they keep the fires going all night!

The next morning, Tom was just as happy as could be dragging that cast in the snow. It had snowed about two inches that night. That meant all signs would be fresh.

There must have been more elk coming out of the park, as there were signs everywhere. Later on that day we ran into the biggest bull I had seen in a long time, but my hunter could not get off his horse fast enough to get a shot. We rode over to Mudd Lake and saw a herd of about forty head. There was one spike in the bunch, but my hunter had decided not to take the spike. He looked so small after seeing the big one.

It was a clear day but colder than heck. We decided to work our way back to camp and have our lunch by the fire. When we got there, Tom and his hunters were already there. His hunter, Dennis, had gotten a five-point. Slim came into camp and one of his hunters had gotten a spike. All of us had seen quite a few elk that day.

There seemed to be more elk around than I had seen in some time. We had been in camp for a couple of hours when Tom came in. His hunter, Doc, had shot a seven-point bull. That was something worth having a Camp Special over! By now, Tom's cast had crumbled and come off up to his ankle, but didn't seem to bother him much. He was still laughing and joking around with everyone. He and his hunters got a couple of pack horses and went to get that big elk. Nighttime came and no Tom and his hunters. Slim came in and they had another elk. It looked like we were going to have a 100% kill before it was all over.

At midnight Tom still hadn't come in. I was quite sure that Tom could take care of himself and his hunters. Bob, Slim, and I decided to hit the hay. About three in the morning we heard the damndest noise. Tom was singing so loud that he woke the whole camp up.

He had come to camp dragging his hunters behind him. We got up and went out to see if everything was all right. Old Tom was drunker than a five-legged billy goat, and his two hunters were frozen to their saddles. Tom had a bottle of beer in each hand and was trying to tell Bob and me about the big elk they got, when he fell off his horse head first in the snow. We picked him up, got him on his feet, and then went over to help his hunters.

They needed the help! Old Doc couldn't turn loose of the saddle horn—his hands were frozen around it. Then, when we did get him off, his legs would not work! He said his knee joints had frozen stiff, and poor Dennis couldn't talk because his teeth were chattering too hard. They both had beer in their pockets and saddlebags, and Tom was dragging his cast around, doing a little war dance, saying to Doc and Dennis, "Boy, didn't we have fun? We sure had fun!" Doc looked at him and shook his head

164

and mumbled some kind of a swear word and a bunch of buffalo chips. Then, we got them in the cook tent and thawed them out.

Tom didn't seem to be overly cold or in any pain. After they got a couple cups of coffee down them, the first thing Doc said was, "I just had the wildest experience of my life in the wildest country in the world, and with the wildest Indian in the country. But, he has to be the best guide I have ever seen!"

They said that after they left camp to pick up the seven-point bull, they got down to where Lava Creek crosses the trail at the base of Gravel Mountain. There they came upon a herd of elk and, lo and behold, it had a seven-point bull with them, and Tom got him. I have seen a couple when I was guiding, but you don't shoot an elk from under your hunter's nose. But, their guide had a broken leg and a cast that was about to fall off . . . anyway, after they had cleaned Tom's elk it was getting dark, and Tom said, "Come on boys, this calls for a drink!" and away they went. His two hunters thought he he was heading for camp. Little did they know what lay ahead!

Old Tom headed down country, singing and telling the hunters stories; that seemed to make their fourteen-mile ride a little shorter. Old Tom was headed for Mary's Place. Mary had a little bar that was named something like Buffalo Ranch. When they got there they tied the horses to the uprights on the porch and went in. Tom ordered drinks for all. After they had a couple, the hunters wanted to leave, but Tom just kept right on till Mary closed the place. Tom got all the beer he could get in their saddlebags and in his and the hunters' pockets, and up the trail they went, Tom leading and just singing like a magpie.

Well, these hunters thought they were going to freeze to death before they got to camp. It was around seven below zero. They had left the pack horses tied up by the big elk Tom had shot and when they came by, they turned them loose so they could go to camp. That was the first time the hunters knew where they were. They were damn thankful to get back to camp, and they sure had one hell of an experience!

It takes a special kind of person to be a guide. When I was outfitting, top pay was fifteen to twenty dollars a day. Today it is forty to fifty dollars a day. The guide's job varies depending on the outfit he is working for, helping to get the gear ready for hunting season, packing the camp in, helping set up camp, digging out the watering hole, chopping wood, riding the young horses that aren't broken, taking care of his and the hunter's horses (saddling and unsaddling, feeding, watering, and rubbing them down), putting up the tents, building corrals, putting in an outhouse, knowing how to field-dress game and how to skin and quarter them, packing meat on a horse, cleaning out trails, reading trail blazes, reading game signs, tracking game when wounded, knowing how to throw a diamond on an old pack horse, making sure the packs are balanced, knowing how much weight a horse can carry, tailing up a pack string, knowing how long and what kind of knot to tie, finding his way in the mountains, day or night, and knowing and respecting the game laws.

In camp, a guide's day starts about five in the morning and ends sometime after dark. He has no union to back him up, no starting or stopping time, no assistance from the government, no insurance. If he got union pay with overtime, within a few years he would own the ranch!

I have heard comments said about guides: he must have been kicked by a mule; run over by a buffalo herd, a freight train, and a herd of wild horses; stomped on; kicked in the head; thrown off a horse; born with no brains; dragged behind a horse; or dropped off a cliff! I have known older guides that have retired from guiding, outfitting, and packing like my old friend, Joe Back, that sure felt at times that they have been "rode awfully hard and put away wet." But, if you put his kind in a big city, with all the asphalt, big buildings, traffic in every direction, and where the pool hall is about the only recreation, within a year he would go stark, raving mad.

Well, Pardner, I'll let you in on a little secret. He loves those mountains, those deep canyons, the snow on those peaks, the deep, misty black timber, and those beautiful meadows. He may have red or blonde hair, but he still has a little Indian in him. He can feel nature in and all around him and always has that craving to see what's on the other side of the mountain. And he damn sure loves a good saddle horse and that magnificent, beautiful game that roams through these breathtaking mountains of Wyoming.

Thanks, Joe

At the age of 86, Joe would still rather quit the gas wagon and leave all electricity behind and look at the real world with a good horse under him. I've always been greatly taken with people who could enjoy the little, everyday things of life and can give of themselves warmly and sincerely.

Years ago Joe taught me how to sculpt. At the time he hardly knew me, but he took the time, had the patience, and enjoyed doing it. That's the way Joe is.

Now, there aren't too many men left who savvy how it is to ride a horse all day at twenty or thirty degrees below to take care of stock; after guiding all day, come into camp, gather up five or six pack horses and a fresh saddle horse to pack the game meat out twelve or fifteen miles with just the moonlight for help; be back in camp by two or three in the morning, unsaddle and feed the ponies; be in bed by four and up by five to get the hunter out by daylight; then guide all day again.

Funny cusses, horses. If you spend much of your life handling a string of them, you're bound to get some bruises or broken bones to show for it. Joe has been kicked, stomped on, thrown off, and a horse has even rolled over on him. Then, he will sit around the campfire and tell stories with high regard and affection about his string of horses. I suppose that's what it takes to be a real guide and outfitter. Now, if some city folks got his wages, ate his grub, and bedded down in a snowbank in his bedroll, they would damn sure wonder how and why he thanked God every day for the life he lived and called his "romance."

Thanks, Joe, for the privilege of letting me put my gatherings in your book. When I first started it, it was like trying to pull a tooth out of a biting, kicking, striking, lop-eared Government mule! But after I got through the first stories, it got me to remembering and I started writing

167

and chuckling to myself. I tried to put it down pretty straight, but I did put in a *little* kibosh here and there. I would not bet my Sunday socks that folks will not want to read my part of the book, but if they do, I sure hope that they get a little belly laugh out of it.

A lot of the hunters we have had, who make their livings in the big city, kind of remind us of ourselves. We are all human and come from the same kind of molds. I know my "paper talk" manners are not much. I have had but little book learning. I am not what you could call an educated twentieth-century manicured cowboy. I guess I've been cut out of a different string.

Joe, one of the losses of my life was not being old enough to hunt and guide with you. Maybe in later years, if the Good Lord has a place up there that is somewhere close to Wyoming we can throw a diamond hitch on an old pony and ride some rocky trails together. God Bless, keep a leg on each side, and never say quit!